The Post-Modern Aura

The Post-Modern Aura

The Act of Fiction
in an Age of Inflation

By Charles Newman

with a Preface by Gerald Graff

Northwestern University Press

Evanston

1985

Published by Northwestern University Press
All Rights Reserved
No portion of this book may be reproduced without
written permission of the Publisher.

An earlier version of this text appeared
in *Salmagundi,* Vol. 63-64, 1984; reprinted with permission.

ISBN #   Cloth 0-8101-0668-X, Paper 0-8101-0669-8
Library of Congress Catalog Card Number 84-61438

Printed in USA

for Mrs. Schweinhundt,
the one and only

Contents

The Post-Modern Aura

Preface

Charles Newman's *The Post-Modern Aura* is a highly original critique of the pretensions of the literary-cultural Avant-Garde in the United States today. It is also a critique of the current opposition to the Avant-Garde — neo-realists, academic humanists, and political conservatives. It is more than a negative critique, however, for in showing why these opposing positions are inadequate, Newman presents a persuasive analysis of what he describes as an Age of Inflation. It is the paradoxical dynamics of "inflation," a word Newman uses both as a narrowly economic and a broadly cultural concept, which neither traditionalists nor cultural revolutionaries have understood. Whatever their differences, both groups still believe the conflict between "tradition" and "radical" subversion is a live issue in contemporary American culture, whereas Newman argues that an inflationary culture makes it a pseudo-issue.

Of course, in any discussion such as this, a great deal depends on what is meant by words like "radical," "Avant-Garde," and "tradition," to say nothing of "contemporary American culture," as well as all the other terms making up the currency in which debates over questions of culture are conducted. And it is one of Newman's points that this intellectual-conceptual "currency" has become as inflated as the American dollar here and abroad. Much of the fascination of Newman's analysis, in fact, comes from his keen recognition that the corruption which he is writing *about* necessarily infects the words in which his analysis has to be made — most notably the word "Post-Modern" itself. The word has been used so pretentiously and self-servingly that it is difficult to take the concept seriously yet not easy to dismiss it. For to the intellectual historian, the law of mind over matter must be honored: once a certain number of people *believe* that a concept like the Post-Modern marks a real change in the cultural climate, that change *becomes* a reality to be reckoned with, even if the reality is not exactly what most users of the term think it is.

Newman's book, like the Post-Modern works of fiction and art it describes (and like Newman's own accomplished fiction) is therefore one of those "self-conscious" texts which call attention to the inadequacy of the linguistic elements of which they are made. Yet unlike a lot of that fiction and art, Newman's argument never simply cancels itself or engages in the kind of protective ironic cop-out which relieves the writer from having to take responsibility for his position. Perhaps this helps explain how Newman manages to present a serious and constructive argument while being very funny, and to shift his registers of discourse, moving rapidly — sometimes within the same sentence — between the high talk of cultural analysts like Benjamin, Adorno, and Canetti and the low talk of publishing economics, or mixing the concepts of literary theory with those of baseball. Newman recognizes that one of the constituents of a Post-Modern culture is the license to talk about anything in the context of anything else, for where international banking has become more surrealist than Surrealist art, older categories of relevance cease to apply.

Here, unfortunately, is where Newman's critique is likely to pass over the heads of those Avant-Gardists to whom he addresses much of his argument. They will no doubt react as they always do when attacked, which is to cry "reactionary" and "traditionalist," and to claim that the critic must be speaking for the forces of "repression." In other words, they will haul out the very arsenal of terms and oppositions which Newman is calling into question, for it is only by doing so that the Avant-Garde can avoid having to rethink the position in which it has invested. Indeed, this counterattack on Newman has already begun — in the pages of *Salmagundi* in which an earlier version of Newman's book (extensively revised in the present edition) first appeared.

Of course anyone is free to quarrel with Newman's contention that in the new situation of contemporary culture, the real problem is no longer public *repression* of advanced art but public *indifference*. What is pathetic about the Avant-Garde's reaction is its inability even to recognize the possibility of such a state of affairs, so that anybody who suggests it must be a neoconservative. Yet in a certain sense Newman is a truer loyalist to the Avant-Garde than its publicists and professional promoters, since he takes it seriously enough to be worth arguing with.

In fact the whole tenor of Newman's book is finally "progressive" in the best sense rather than pessimistic, fatalistic, or nostalgic. It is not a call for "moral fiction" or for the shoring up of cultural traditions or for "humanistic values." Nor is it a Marxist analysis, though its argument owes something to the Marxist recognition that art has a social basis, for it accepts the fact that consumer capitalism is not likely to disappear within our lifetime. Newman believes that "the act of fiction" can recover its latent dignity and become a major influence in American culture, and he thinks that if we can set aside certain false diagnoses which turn the problem into a hopeless metaphysical quandary inherent in the Death of the Word, positive things can be done. Much depends for Newman on the economics of publishing, a topic which, as Christopher Lasch has admiringly pointed out, is hardly ever addressed by literary criticism. Newman does not claim to have all the answers for the predicament of fiction today, but his inquiry figures to move the discussion of the problem in a more useful direction.

— *Gerald Graff*

I feel very twentieth-century and not at all modern.
—Ortega y Gasset

Foreword

No longer is it, 'When I hear the word Culture, I reach for my revolver.' We are permitted instead, 'Culture sits so well in my pocket that whenever I hear the word "thought" I smile.'
— *Philippe Sollers*

As befits its subject, this will be a brief account of an incomplete idea; nothing so juicy as a sensibility, only a dim pathology of the contemporary, which amounts to Art is everywhere and Life is vague. The "Post-Modern" is neither a canon of writers, nor a body of criticism, though it is often applied to literature of, roughly, the last twenty years. The very term signifies a simultaneous continuity and renunciation, a generation strong enough to dissolve the old order, but too weak to marshall the centrifugal forces it has released. This new literature founders in its own hard won heterogeneity, and tends to lose the sense of itself as a human institution. My account is accordingly a survey of attitudes and tendencies, gestures and drifts, alibis and advertisements, clichés and obfuscations, which comprise an institution without a theory.

"Post-Modernism" in its positive form constitutes an intellectual attack upon the atomized, passive and indifferent mass culture which, through the saturation of electronic technology, has reached its zenith in Post-War America. The reaction in the 1950's against the falsity and meretriciousness of this culture was expressed through ironic detachment, characterized by a contemplative indifference to politics, the conservation of valued cultural objects in all their complexity, and the missionary spirit associated with late Modernism. The critical faculty was elevated as the saving remnant of civilization, implying that experience could still be satisfying if ordered in literary terms.

The Sixties would of course emphasize the subversive rather than the positive socializing function of literature, a resurrection, almost exclusively, of early Modernist avant-garde attitudes. What is striking about this period is not so much the politicalization of aesthetic man; for all its rejection of "elitist" art, the Sixties produced no enduring innovation in aesthetics, and for all its 'revolutionary' enthusiasm, its politics were literary and second hand. One is reminded a bit of *fin de siècle* Vienna, which produced an extraordinary number of "movements," as well as a hyperpluralistic social order which was only the prelude to total political and cultural disarray.

What *was* unprecedented in the Sixties was the astonishingly rapid shift made by intellectuals from the private sensibility of an "armed" criticism to the politics and art of "immediacy and openness." The period established a rotational dynamic which would be repeated in different idioms but with similar lack of effect up to the present day. It is the *velocity* of this change, in both art and criticism, rather than its substantive merits, which is the distinctive feature of the "Post-Modern." For it is a weary truism of literary physics that conventional mechanics cannot explain phenomena in which motions of very high velocity play a role. The concept of generation, that residue of traditional evidence which undergoes a transformation coherent enough to be periodized, has been gradually foreshortened from three score to the decade, and even this new shorthand is probably too inclusive.

There is a more elemental way of regarding Post-Modernism, however, and that is in terms of *climax inflation* — not only of wealth, but of people, ideas, methods, and expectations — the increasing power and pervasiveness of the communications industry, the reckless growth of the academy, the incessant changing of hands and intrinsic devaluation of all received ideas. The Post-Modern era represents only the last phase in a century of inflation — when it becomes structurally permanent in the longest sustained economic rocket ride since the industrial revolution, arguably the most explosive period of sustained growth in human history.

The effects are by now clear even to the most literary mind. Chronic excess demand fosters irrational consumption; all goods, intellectual as well as material, become nondurable, buying and selling take precedence over production and investment. Rather than a genuinely productive wealth, a patrimony which can be passed on, chronic inflation increasingly produces only hedges against inflation and distortions of the market, which is to say, it fosters cultural incoherence of the most destructive sort. As inflation affects members of the community unequally, alienation is intensified, consensus unravels, the trade unionist mentality permeates all levels of society, the social order becomes a war of group against group for decreasing shares of the national income, and the skepticism of *all* forms of governance intensifies. Power flows to those institutions which can take on the highest debt. The old saw, "everybody floats, nobody drowns," takes on almost metaphysical quality. In a little more than a generation, our population has almost doubled, per capita income has increased 1,000%, college enrollment has increased 7 times. Our total gross national product is up more than 2,200%, as is personal spending, as we have undergone an unprecedented global price revolution since World War II of 300-600%, depending upon which commodity index is used. The dollar, which was halved in value from 1946-1969, was halved again in the last decade — a trebling of consumer prices reflecting the worst inflation in the history of the Republic.

The fatalism of *anticipated* inflation which these statistics reflect, the failure of prices to conform to past experience and the consequent inability to determine any stable theory of *value*, can only be fully grasped historically — particularly in a year in which we have seemingly regained some control over prices. While wholesale prices have been gradually rising since 1932, it is also true that their averaged index of 1932 had not risen substantially since *1832*. Indeed, the wholesale price peak of 1796 was not consistently exceeded, except during the wars, until 1947. In this context, the entire 19th Century was actually mildly deflationary, and beginning in 1800, every deflation has been sharper and briefer than the last, while each successive inflation has been sharper and longer. The inflation we have experienced since our Asian War (for which we will be paying for the rest of our lives) may justly recall the 16th Century, when the influx of American "treasure" coincided with the commercialization of trade to produce a devaluation of most European currencies.

This is not, however, an argument based on economic determinism. Inflation is a cultural malaise of genuinely moral dimensions, with psychological causes and economic symptoms. It constitutes an intractable and insidious social phenomenon which will not submit to contemporary preferences for solution by technique. Despite the fact that inflation occurs historically in only brief bursts, it leaves an indelible impression and creates incalculable uncertainty, a negative sum game in which all participants ultimately lose. What is lost is not purchasing power *per se*. The ever increasing price revolution only disturbed confidence very recently, because it was not as severe as the hyperinflations which followed total military disasters, as with the Confederate States or Weimar Germany. America's memory of economic chaos is one of unemployment rather than hyperinflation. The causes of this are obviously manifold, but what is clear is that the instabilities of the system which once produced depression now seem to manifest themselves in inflation. The effect is that all the latent disequilibriums of a market system which is allocatively efficient precisely because it is devoid of values, are further exacerbated through inflation, which weakens all reciprocal relationships in a society never notable for cohesion. The trivialization of culture and the psychological tensions which always attend a market economy reach new levels of carelessness when no one dares to abate consumption. Neither the competitive market nor the political process can operate with an authority sufficient to clear the market or to reconcile its interests. In late capitalism, inflation does not produce political havoc, but cultural anomie. Elias Canetti has written:

> The confusion inflation wreaks on the population is by no means confined to the actual period of inflation . . . apart from wars and revolutions, there is nothing in our modern civilizations which compares in importance to it. The upheavals are so profound that people prefer to hush them up and conceal them . . . [it is] infinitely shaming . . . growth negates itself; as the crowd grows, its units become weaker and weaker . . . not only is everything shaken . . . but each man, each person becomes less . . . Everyone has a million and everyone is nothing . . . No one ever forgets a sudden depreciation of himself, for it is too painful . . . the natural tendency afterwards is to find something which is worth even less than oneself, which one can even despise as one was despised oneself . . . What is wanted is a dynamic process of humiliation. . . . *[Crowds and Power]*

For Post-Moderns, inflation is our war *and* revolution, and art often our humiliation.

Inflation affects the ideas exchange just as surely as it does commercial markets. In those areas not completely ruled by short term supply and demand, such as Art, the velocity of change may be compared to that in those "underdeveloped" nations, which in a generation undergo historical changes which formerly took hundreds of years to accomplish. Thus we are witness to continual internecine warfare and spasmodic changes in fashion, the simultaneous display of all past styles in their infinite mutations, and the continuous circulation of diverse and contradictory intellectual elites, which signal the reign of the cult of *creativity* in all areas of behavior, an unprecedented nonjudgmental receptivity to Art, a tolerance which finally amounts only to indifference. To put it in less theoretical terms, one recalls with awe Edmund Wilson's seemingly telepathic sense in choosing which of 8,000 annual new titles to review during his Thirties' tenure at the *New Republic*. One wonders how he would have done with the current 55,000 annual titles. In the last thirty years, more novels have been published than in any comparable period of history, and yet, quality aside, no age has been less sure about what a novel *is*, or more skeptical of the value and function of "imaginative" literature.

The effect of this proliferation of knowledge has a longer tradition than we generally admit. "Scarcely anyone in the 'educated classes,' " writes Matthew Arnold, "seems to have any real opinions, or places any faith in those which he professes to have . . . it requires in these times much more intellect to marshall so much greater a stock of ideas and observations . . . Those who should be guides for the rest, see too many sides to every question. They hear so much said, and find that so much can be said, about everything, that they feel no assurance about anything."

The overwhelming sense not merely of the relativity of ideas, but of the sheer quantity and incoherence of information, a culture of inextricable cross-currents and energies — such is *the* primary sensation of our time. The majority of books in most libraries were published in the last thirty years. Seldom has the mind been burdened by so many competing claims, and never has Art taken place in so many spheres amidst so many competing vested interests. We are dealing here not with the fragmentation at first so lovingly approved and finally despaired of by the Modernist Movement, but with presumptive special interests (systems would be too dignified) which have no explicable relation. The pluralism of contemporary art parallels the increasingly sectarian divisions of society. There can be no triumph of a style, or for that matter an interpretation, in a situation lacking any principle of succession. The lens turned on contemporary art must allow for all distortions. Art refuses to flow into the old channels, just as technology simultaneously destroys and opens new ones, the consequences of which no one fully comprehends. The Post-Modern is above all characterized by the *inflation of discourse*, manifesting itself in literature through the illusion that technique can remove itself from history by attacking a concept of objective reality which has already faded from the world, and in criticism by the development of secondary languages which presumably "demystify" reality, but actually tend to further obscure it. In such a situation, both the critical and the aesthetic intelligence often relinquish their traditional claims, preferring to explore what they imagine to be the richness of their own limitations.

Modernism fully corroborated the romantic notion that Art could be destructive as well as uplifting. It is our very contemporary discovery that art can trivialize, benumb as well as enlarge our experience, and that precisely at the moment when the potential public for art is greater than ever before, the artist finds himself both voluntarily rejecting and being refused access to a contemporary audience, a reciprocally destructive inertia. Modernism kept alive the nostalgia for an art which would retain the social and moral authority of religion and even empire — an authority destroyed as artists became simply other producers for the marketplace. But the relationship between producers and consumers reaches a new level of irreducible complexity when the artist must do battle on two fronts: against official mass culture as well as Pseudo-Art. It is a central point of mine that whereas the Modern and the Post-Modern share an unbroken (and largely unexamined) aesthetic tradition, their differences in idiom are due essentially to the differences of the institutions against which they are reacting. Which is to say that Post-Modernism is defined by the confusion which comes from bringing forth the dogmatic aesthetic techniques of Modernism against an entirely unprecedented form of production, transmission and administration of knowledge, a system no less binding because it is unstructured (what Hans Enzensberger calls "the Consciousness Industry"). Modernism in its heroic phase is a retrospective revolt against a retrograde mechanical industrialism. Post-Modernism is an ahistorical rebellion without heroes against a blindly innovative information society.

Walter Benjamin anticipates the peculiar relentless fluidity of the roles in our new writer/reader system. "With the increasing extension of the press, an increasing number of readers became writers . . . thus the distinction between author and public is about to lose its basic character . . . The difference becomes merely functional; it may vary from case to case, but at any moment, the reader is ready to turn into a writer . . . literary license is now founded on polytechnic rather than specialized training and thus becomes common property." The case is summarily adumbrated by Sartre: "The drastic blurring of levels in the public since 1848 has caused the author initially to write against all readers . . . The fundamental conflict between the writer and the reader is an unprecedented phenomenon in the history of literature."

This intransigence has been reflected most often in the notion of a permanent crisis in art, sometimes treated as purifying, sometimes as stultifying, but always as unending and eschatological. But if we have learned anything from our forty year detente, it is that crisis is not inherent in the moment itself, that our thinking is skewed by apocalyptic rhetoric, no matter how irresolute and plastic our art may be, or how undeniable the ongoing rot of our social, political and economic institutions. Indeed, the inflated rhetoric of crisis more often than not dovetails nicely with the commercial rhetoric of calculated obsolescence, the continual tremors of the fashion world. Our society retains a remarkable ability to absorb its severest critiques and even make a profit on them. What the artist expresses as metaphysical or linguistic alienation is often nothing more or less than his hypertrophied social and economic isolation, or in the case of celebrity, his exploitation. The artist is rarely an unpopular commodity in the abstract. It is only when he must find a specific place in the productive relations of his society that he tends to fall back upon the nostalgic and easily purchased notions of Modernist Transcendence. The rhetoric of crisis tends to release the artist from the constraints of history and revolution, and is characteristically expressed in the style of Formalist involution. This has in turn occasioned a recent return to a kind of neo-conservative Realism, or Literal Revivalism. Post-Modernism has then come to represent the final battle in the century's war of attrition between Formalism and Realism, those totally aestheticized antinomies shorn of their historical context — a violent adjacency of the idols of pure expressivity and pure accessibility, which reflect more often than not an atmosphere of intense demoralization.

After a century of ineluctable crisis, we dimly apprehend that the emergency is not likely to resolve itself apocalyptically or even neatly; we are at one of those historic junctures where we can only wonder how our common sense was beaten out of us. Imagine a 20th century without jargon! It is the very rhetoric of crisis itself which offends any plausible sense of continuity, and prevents us from dealing with what turn out to be genuinely unprecedented circumstances. And it is my point that the Artist has failed to understand that ahistoricism like any *de facto* liberation has its own considerable risks, that his peculiar blend of assertion and denial does not exist apart from the complex tensions of society, and that his vague attitudes towards History, Adversary, Genre and Audience tend to determine his working options. The making and experiencing of fiction remains a critical/historical act, no matter how bankrupt critical and historical categories may be, and no matter how ingenuously the artist may deny them. Technique, no less than empathy, remains a *learned* response. The artist has only special solutions; his problems are commonplace. To write against the reader is a social as much as literary phenomenon; isolation is not so much a universal condition as a specific social fate.

My biases and preferences ought to be clear. My notions about fiction do not derive from any organic view of literature or society, much less from any methodology, but from a struggle with my own work, and an unsystematic but always instructive acquaintanceship with my contemporaries. I am a Formalist in the sense that I believe works of art to be first-order phenomena, not cultural reflections or by-products, but I am a Realist in the sense that I hold the pose of autonomy, the tendency to shrug off any reciprocal relations, so much the contemporary fashion, to be a sham. And while technique is indeed the crucial determinant of literary quality, I believe that if style is not the man, precisely, it can only be achieved by a vivid and intensely personal experience of life. This should seem less contradictory by the end of this study.

I also tend to see cultural and aesthetic conflicts as explicably social and economic, though in neither dialectical nor materialist terms. When I refer to art, I am talking almost exclusively about literature. When I speak of literature I am almost always talking about fiction. This is complicated by the fact that there is no such thing as a Post-Modern canon. Contemporary writers are uniquely different from one another, and any exemplary paragraph in support of a generalization from one could easily be countered with another. While there are many admirable writers to whom my generalities will not apply, I have tried to sketch a literary dynamic in which broad aesthetic choices can be understood in a specific cultural circumstance. I have tried to avoid the partisan, but I make no pretense at being fair. The argument is unapologetically general; what I have left out is not inadvertent. In any case, true exceptions will eventually turn out to be far more significant than any rule I presently manage. But if there is no body of ideas so elegant as to constitute a true *Zeitgeist*, there are, it seems to me, a number of shared questions and feelings, abortive procedures and mock dead ends, the imperfect digestion of which is well worth illuminating. Obviously, a number of questions are raised to which I cannot offer even the most tentative answer.

As this is a cultural history of recent *attitudes*, rather than a specifically literary argument, there is little textual explication. I am primarily interested in the concepts which hover around artistic transactions, that mismatched intellectual baggage aboard every imaginative flight, the weight of which is only subliminally acknowledged. My point is not to defend contemporary literature as much as to ask why we have made such a poor case for it.

The reader who delights in praise and blame, or who requires a scoreboard for the endless extra-innings of Post-Modernism, will be doubly frustrated. I stick to theory not because I think it conspicuously related to practice or even intrinsically interesting, but because I find contemporary culture so willfully theoretical. This should not be surprising in a culture which is disintegrating, for theory is the only way we know to overcome static self-consciousness and to recontextualize ourselves. An inflationary culture, because its overlapping realities are not only proliferating but cancelling each other out, tends to polarize theories as it recirculates them, and as content itself is being continuously devalued, there is a strong tendency to treat both art and life as abstract models. Accordingly, America has become the new Germany of theory — from sexology to surprise-side economics — promulgated by a corps of academics, preachers, journalists and media hustlers, breathless with fatidic supposition. Even so marginal a group as writers routinely acknowledge theoretical problems which would not have even occurred to practitioners only a generation ago. It requires an enormous effort to ignore, much less refute this conjectural energy. What we have undergone, on the face of it, is a temporary abandonment of traditional American aesthetic pragmatism.

There are several reasons, at least, for this manic flirtation with theory. The first is that after television, the dissemination of theory in America is relatively cost-free, functioning as another market commodity, without the price exacted by ideological conflict in most other cultures. As a Russian friend once remarked to me, "America is the only place left that can afford Marxism.'' Secondly, pragmatism requires relative stability, consensus — a context for negotiation. When a culture is highly volatile and genuinely confused, the art of exigencies is undervalued. Theory becomes an infinitely expendable currency, the ultimate inflation hedge. Theory more than any work of art is most easily translated into Hype, which is the conceptual engine of our overstimulated culture.

My impatience with speculation does not of course prevent me from making a number of blind assertions of my own, and no illustrative example will suffice where the reader is unwilling to apply my generalizations to his own experience. In detecting the inevitable limitations of my argument, I hope we will also appreciate the considerable difficulties involved. Our frailties are never more on display than when we give names to Time.

New York, New York, 1984

I.

1. Meditation on a Lost Nomenclature

Only history can do what it likes.
—*A. Solzhenitsyn*

We should define, should we not, what we mean by history?
—*V. Nabokov*

Ours is a richly confused and hugely verbal age, energized by a multitude of competing discourses, the very proliferation and plasticity of which increasingly determine what we defensively refer to as our reality. We have become acutely aware of language not as a mediating tool, but as an independent agency in its own right, a force which is not an adjunct of perception, but a competitor. Never before in history has so much of a literary heritage been available to so broadly based an audience, yet never before has a culture drawn such apparently meagre sustenance from its own literary activity. With a culture so unsure of itself, the proclamation of endless, unnerving change and insistent uniqueness has been a common response of both American character and literature. This exceptionality is often neither earned nor demonstrated, but, like the corollary of a "birthright," is viewed as *the* artist's prerogative; perhaps his only one. When excellence is not defined, much less rewarded, then to be "different" is the minimal requisite.

Conservative critics often attribute this to pure venality, an unwillingness to impose standards in a culture which wants nothing to do with the business of meritocracy. All of which, of course, is true on the face of it. What is frequently missed, however, is the fact that increasingly over the last thirty years or so, all our literary antecedents have become available to the American writer; he may draw upon a genuine variety of intracultural modes; national character no longer delimits genre; and the notion of genre itself has been radically redefined.

It goes without saying that these are not unmixed blessings. If a Martian were given the punitive task of reading any recent year's

American fiction, he might well conclude that these books were produced by writers not only from different cultures but from different planets. Whatever comparative judgments may eventually accrue to the literature of our age (and we are acutely aware of how we will be judged), no one can dispute its willful and bewildering variety.

We live in a time when no purview is possible. This reflects the inflation of both literary and social expectations as well as a massive restructuring of communications and dealignment of institutions. Inflation affects literary operations and preoccupations quite as much as it does financial scrip. In such a situation, specific polemic takes refuge in quasi-philosophical assertions; both criticism and art tend to adopt a desperately involuted stance, as there is no methodology or even a common public relations which can provide third party coherence.

It is quite unlikely that the nature of literary enterprise has changed radically, but it is nevertheless possible that our attitudes toward it have — and Post-Modernism represents not so much formal innovation in itself as a change in the dynamic between literature and what might quaintly be described as the social order. It signifies a change in the context into which texts are received, a recognition that institutions of transmission substantially alter what is being conveyed, and that institutions are defined in the contemporary world by their breaking points. This embodies a very unpopular notion for American writers in particular, for it suggests that culture, particularly one so "free," determines art in ways that the Modernist tradition of the autonomous artist resists absolutely. In fact, the Post-Modern can be partially understood as a shift in the *choice* of determinisms — a subtle but inexorable movement within two generations from economic and political determinisms, through a broader cultural determinism emphasizing technology and mass psychology, to our recent obsession with a determinism which is essentially linguistic. There is some evidence that the cycle may be starting over, but it is clear that the concept of what is *literary* at any one moment is linked to which determinism is *chosen*.

And so we must deal with terminological fictions such as *Post-Modernism* — and indeed, whatever happened to it? While we must remain extremely skeptical of such terms as descriptive, we should consider that a terminology can have considerable operative power quite apart from the fact that it may be incoherent, contradictory, or even self-serving. Such gropings, premonitions and perversions of both language and history often tell us more about a culture than its highest productions. Thus Post-Modernism may in fact mean something beyond its more semantically febrile versions of Art post-partum, post mortem and postponable — a nomenclature which inevitably calls to mind a band of vainglorious contemporary artists following the circus elephants of Modernism with snow shovels.

The conventional model of Modernism is that of a quantum jump in aesthetic perception — a discreet moment in which the existing decaying culture is definitively thrown off with an explosion of innovation: witness Virginia Woolf's most quoted remark, "on or about December, 1910, human nature changed."

Against the languorous entropy of the Victorian Mind, the Modern Canon stands in sharp summary relief, that ultimate fantasy metaphor of the revolutionary, the spontaneous mutation of historical necessity. According to its central mythology, Modernism was *not* an evolutionary development, but a free radical departure, the evangelical myth of rebirth by fiat. Therein lies its continuous source of appeal to a culture impatient with its own sense of cyclical retrogression and *déjà vu*. While metaphors of gradualism are commonplace in historical and scientific inquiry, they have never been congenial to literary criticism. The fact that the Homo sapiens 50,000 years ago were probably as brainy as we are is not a sentiment upon which to build an Avant-Garde.

Moreover, when a model of creative discontinuity is applied to an historical period, one invites a species of Terroristic Terminology, the sort of vocabulary of which — by contrast with French or German — English was once relatively free. What you get is *Para*-criticism and other fictive prefixes — *Meta, Anti, Super,* and *Sur.*

The explicit emphasis is on a literature which is not only "different," but also *heightened* in some way, as in the Surrealist invocation of a destruction which adds to existence.

Against the botanized categories and closed canons of Modernism, we are dealing with a non-durational history, the banality of endless presentness, the seeing through one's own sight which is the ordering of negative time. Post-Modern is something more than a dash surrounded by a contradiction. It is one of those concepts which must be pursued very deeply to discover how calculatingly superficial it is. Neither pointed like an oxymoron nor soothing like a neologism, it functions as a rhetorical trope, an aposiopetic pause, in which the hyphen is its most distinctive feature — a stutter step, a tenuous graft; the bobbed tale of the hybrid.

How such terminology comes into being is not without interest; it forms the rhetoric of the "not yet categorizable," which is both celebratory and evasive. The idea, as Emerson insisted, is to put distance between the recent and the rigidly canonical. "Our age is retrospective . . . The foregoing generations believed in God and nature face to face; we through their eyes. Why should we not have a poetry and philosophy of insight and not of tradition, and a religion by revelation to us, and not the history of theirs?"

The impulse and trade-offs of such an enterprise can clearly be seen in Roger Fry's coinage of the term "Post-Impressionism," in introducing French Modernism to the British art world of 1910-11. Virginia Woolf noted that Fry thought it quite easy to make the transition from Watts to Picasso; there was no break, only a continuation. *"They were only pushing things a little further,"* she paraphrased him, echoing that respect for the evolutionary in which intonation is everything. Desmond McCarthy in his introduction to the Grafton Exhibit sets the tone for such a transition in his usual half-aggressive, half-apologetic manner.

> . . . there is no denying that the work of the Post Impressionists is sufficiently disconcerting. It may even appear ridiculous to those who do well to recall the fact that a good rockinghorse has often more of the true horse about it than an instantaneous photograph of a derby winner.

This is the insistence of a man who hardly thinks of himself as a revolutionary theorist, but against mindless conventional wisdom is simply asserting the relatively obvious; i.e., that traditional pictorial realism is not the only way to represent reality. We shall see how far that commonplace can be pushed in small increments.

Fry's own position was even more tenuous. At first it seems he wanted to characterize these painters as "Expressionists,"* but at the urging of the press, he came up with a new name — "oh, let's call them Post-Impressionists; at any rate they came after the Impressionists." In his essay "Retrospect," Fry goes on:

---

*The term "Expressionism" seems first to have appeared in 1911, also in the Foreword to a catalog, in this case the 22nd Exhibition of the *Berliner Sezession*. The term characterized a group of young French painters (including Picasso, Braque and Dufy) and was rapidly applied to any painter reacting against "Impressionism."

. . . for purposes of convenience it was necessary to give these artists a name, and I chose, as being the vaguest and most noncommittal, the name of Post Impressionists . . . In conformity with my own previous prejudices against Impressionism, I think I underlined too much their divorce from the parent stock. I see now more clearly their affiliation with it but I was nonetheless right in recognizing their essential difference. . . . The general public failed to see my position with regard to this movement was capable of logical explanation, as the result of a consistent sensibility. I tried in vain to explain what appeared to me so clear, that the modern movement was essentially a return to the ideas of formal design which had been almost lost sight of in the fervent pursuit of naturalistic representation. I found that the cultured public which had welcomed my expositions of the works of the Italian renaissance now regarded me either as incredibly flippant or, for the more charitable explanation which was usually adopted, slightly insane.

In fact the reaction of the "audience" [in this case, "the press"] which so persistently pushed Fry for a new headline nomenclature is more than instructive. In the *London Times* of November 7, 1910, "The Post-Impressionists" are received as follows:

. . . It is lawful to anticipate these critics and to declare our belief that this art is itself a flagrant example of reaction. It professes to simplify and to gain simplicity, it throws away all the long developed skill past artists had acquired and bequeathed. It begins all over again and stops where a child would stop —where is the significance of gesture in the copper colored Tahitian woman lying face downward on a bed and in her strange arms and fingers? Really primitive art is attractive because it is unconscious, but this is deliberate. It is the abandonment of what Goethe called the 'culture conquest' of the past. Like anarchism in politics, it is the rejection of all that civilization has done, the good with the bad . . . there is the Dutch painter Van Gogh with his roughly modeled flowerpieces and his picture of a peasant girl in a green dress so shocking to the normal eye that the effect is plainly meant to recall some of the *dissonances voulués* of Modern music. . . .It is an odd word to use in this gallery, for charm implies a sympathy between themselves and their public and therefore some

concession to what the preface calls contemporary ideals — those
ideals which are never permitted to dictate to the artist what is
beautiful, significant, or worthy to be painted . . . It is the old
story . . . the artist should *épater le bourgeois* . . . such an aim
is most completely realized by the painter Henri Matisse. . . .
Whether it is in any sense great art is a question that may be left
to the decisions of time — *le seul classificateur impeccable.*

Remember that definition of *charm*; for this absence of sympathy
between the artist and his audience is the major *continuity* between
Modernism and Post-Modernism, a destructiveness, if you will, *pushed
just a little bit further*, an almost unconscious escalation of hostilities.

Herbert Read alludes to the basic romantic bourgeois prejudice that
what is painstakingly calculated and developed, highly worked out, in
the sense of consciously altering conventional form, cannot *also* be
deeply felt, at least until that innovation has been certified as a
recognizable "breakthrough," and conceptually assimilated. Obviously,
we can always measure a work against the ideas that
conceptualize/advertise it; what is more difficult is finally to see that
the concept may be more interesting than the work, or that the work
may have only the most tenuous relationship with its conceptualization.
We are all suckers for statements *about* culture — which is not
surprising when the culture, at first glance, seems so balefully
homogeneous, but upon closer inspection, is so unappealingly atomized.
A new "angle" is invariably more charismatic, more assimilable,
handier in every way than the work which presumably springs from
it. And it is no secret that the most honorific concepts are generated
after the fact.

Terroristic Terminology is coextensive with the rise of Journalism
and The Academy as the most powerful mediating institutions in the
culture. As Journalism becomes electronic and all-pervasive, it creates
Buzz-Words, litanies so open-ended as to defeat specificity, but whose
aura creates in the spectator a non-existent actuality. As the Academy
becomes peripheral, its terminology becomes hermetic and privatized,
gestures of autonomy without content, a loss of meaning long since
automatized into a formula. Like Spinoza's substance, Terminology
is the den from which no tracks return. Vocabulary becomes a substitute
for thought. Post-Modern man comes to live in relation to *terms*.

The etymology of Post-Modernism has a longer history than one would expect. The earliest sacerdotal usage seems to appear, of all places, in Toynbee's *The Study of History*, Vol. #9.

A post-Modern age of Western history which opened in the seventh and eighth decades of the nineteenth century had seen the rhythm of a modern Western war and peace cycle broken, in the course of its fourth beat, by the portent of one general war following hard at the heels of another, with an interval of only 25 years between the outbreaks in 1939 and 1914 from 1792 and 1792 from 1672.

Elsewhere Toynbee seems to associate Post-Modernism with the displacement of the characteristic middle class Western moment by the rise of an urban working class. But essentially what Toynbee calls Post-modern is what cultural historians generally call Modern.

The problem is further complicated by the fact that Modernism itself is hardly a clear term, though at least in hindsight we can in most respects differentiate what is romantic from what is modern. The word can be used with some precision to denote certain literary and painterly techniques from, say, 1905 to 1925, but where it ends nobody knows. Furthermore, as Claudio Guillén points out, "our vocabulary in the area of literary history is extremely limited. Nine-tenths of the critical historian's lexicon is of use to the critic but not the historian." [*Literature as System*] Let us consider some examples.

Postmodernism grew out of modern architecture in much the same way mannerist architecture grew out of the high Renaissance, as a partial inversion and modification of the former language of architecture . . . like its progenitor, the movement is committed to engaging current issues, to changing the present, but unlike the avant garde, it does away with the notion of continual innovation or incessant revolution . . . in its attention to historical memory and local context, it also takes a positive approach towards metaphorical buildings, the vernacular, and a new ambiguous kind of space. (Charles Jencks)

"Kaddish" is a work of art in the modernist sense, with characters and a plot; "Howl" is Postmodernist, a direct expression of the writer's personality. (Louis Simpson)

Post modernist art continues the Modernist's critique of traditional mimetic art and shares the Modernists' commitment to innovation, but pursues these aims by methods of its own. It tries to go beyond Modernism as it does Anti-Modernism . . . it tends to be very much a hit or miss affair. (David Lodge)

Finally I should point out that I shall use the term Postmodernism as a convenient phrase for summarizing the poetry I study, even if it leads to absurd consequences like the need to define a Post-Postmodernism. I do so because the term already has some critical weight, and because the poets I study define their enterprise as essentially the creation of an alternative to high Modernism. (Joe David Bellamy)

I end this . . . by not letting you or myself forget what these editors of *Moby Dick* have so outrageously neglected to mention, that the man who more and more stands up as one man of this century to be put with Melville, Dostoevsky, and Rimbaud (men who engage themselves with modern reality in such fierceness and pity as to be of real use to any of us who want to take on the Postmodern) is D.H. Lawrence. (Charles Olson)

Postmodern Literature moves in nihilistic play or mystic transcendence, towards the vanishing point . . . the most intriguing art of our time seems bent on 'unmaking' itself for the sense of making itself anew. (Ihab Hassan)

It matters little who these writers are, only that each of their usages is utterly different. One rarely finds the word Post-Modern used in disciplines in which there is not a canonical structure to attack or dismiss. One does not find it in economics because economists take a more evolutionary view, calling themselves either neo-conservatives or even neo-liberals, and one never sees it in cinematic criticism, where there is no overwhelming sense of history. It pervades art and dance criticism because the specific hegemony of Abstract Expressionism and Balanchine's Neo-classicism are so decisive that Post-Modern becomes a neologism for what one is *not* talking about. Its use is restricted to fields such as architecture where Modernism is understood to be a *totally canonized phenomenon*; an indisputable and inescapable monument.

"Once a book is fathomed," Lawrence has said, "its meaning fixed or established, it is dead." The problem of course with the dead is their legacies, or as Allen Warren Friedman puts it more mildly, "every artist is different from his predecessors because he knows more, but of course, *they* are what he knows. Yet surely this will not satisfy where modern art is concerned, for in a sense, some modern artists have asserted their own validity by implying that their predecessors are precisely what they *do not know*." [*Forms of British Fiction*]

Actually, by the turn of the century, the word 'Modern' had been largely displaced by "isms," and there were three identifiable stages in the evolution of such terms. The first is the recognition that new forces must be named and defined: "a particular coloring of the soul which literary technicians have not so far found to be chemically analysible, and consequently has no name . . . Expressionism today is in the air. . ." [Ivan Goll]. The second is the stage when the vocabulary becomes *aimed* at the press: "I really don't care any more than you do about the word 'Naturalism' . . . however, I repeat it over and over again because things need to be baptized so that the public will regard them as new . . ." [Émile Zola]. The third is when the term becomes part of common usage, vapid intellectualization, and individual artists begin to disassociate themselves from a history which is "owned."

We are now somewhere between the second and third stages.

* * * *

For present practical purposes, we may say that Modernism begins on a still afternoon in 1852 as Flaubert writes Louise Colet, as always at length:

> If I haven't written sooner in reply to your sorrowful and discouraged-sounding letter, it is because I have been in a great fit of work. The day before yesterday I went to bed at five in the morning and yesterday at three. Since last Monday I have put everything else aside, and have done nothing all week but sweat over my Bovary, disgruntled at making such slow progress. I have now reached my ball, which I will begin Monday. I hope that it may go better. Since you last saw me I have written 25 pages in all (25 pages in six weeks). They are tough. Tomorrow I shall read them to Bouillhet. As for myself, I have gone over them so much, recopied them, changed them, handled them, that for the time being I can't make head or tail of them. But I think they will stand

up. You speak of your discouragements: if you could see mine!
Sometimes I don't understand why my arms don't drop from my
body with fatigue, why my brains don't melt away. I am leading
a stern existence, stripped of all external pleasure, and am
sustained only by a kind of permanent rage, which sometimes
makes me weep tears of impotence but which never abates. I love
my work with a love that is frenzied and perverted, as an ascetic
loves the hair shirt that scratches his belly. Sometimes, when I
am empty, when words don't come, when I find I haven't written
a single sentence after scribbling whole pages, I collapse on my
couch and lie there dazed, bogged in a swamp of despair, hating
myself and blaming myself for this demented pride which makes
me pant after a chimera. A quarter of an hour later everything
changes; my heart is pounding with joy. Last Wednesday I had
to get up and fetch my handkerchief; tears were streaming down
my face. I had been moved by my own writing; the emotion I
had conceived, the phrase that rendered it, and the satisfaction
of having found the phrase — all those elements were present in
this emotion, which after all was predominantly a matter of
nerves. There exist even higher emotions of this same kind: those
which are devoid of the sensory element. These are superior, in
moral beauty, to virtue — so independent are they of any personal
factor, of any human implication. Occasionally (at general
moments of illumination) I have had glimpses, in the glow of an
enthusiasm that made me thrill from head to foot, of such a state
of mind, superior to life itself, a state in which fame counts for
nothing and even happiness is superfluous. If everything around
us, instead of permanently conspiring to drown us in a slough
of mud, contributed rather to keep our spirits healthy, who can
tell whether we might not be able to do for aesthetics what stoicism
did for morals? . . . . Greek art was not an art; it was the very
constitution of an entire race, of the country itself. . .

The time for Beauty is over. Mankind may return to it, but it
has no use for it at present. The more Art develops, the more
scientific it will be, just as science will become artistic. Separated
in their early stages, the two will become one again when both
reach their culmination. It is beyond the power of human thought
today to foresee in what a dazzling intellectual light the works
of the future will flower. Meanwhile we are in a shadowy corridor,

groping in the dark. We are without a lever; the ground is slipping under our feet; we all lack a basis — literati and scribblers that we are. What's the good of all this? Is our chatter the answer to any need? Between the crowd and ourselves no bond exists. Alas for the crowd; alas for us, especially. But since there is a reason for everything, and since the fancy of one individual seems to me just as valid as the appetite of a million men and can occupy an equal place in the world, we must (regardless of material things and of mankind, which disavows us) live for our vocation, climb into our ivory tower, and dwell there along with emptiness — doubts that taunt me at my moments of naivest satisfaction. And yet I would not exchange all this for anything, because my conscience tells me that I am fulfilling my duty, obeying a decree of fate — that I am doing what is Good, that I am in the Right . . .

Clearly all the basic assumptions and contradictions of Modernism are already in place:

The certitude of despair.

Aesthetic (and ascetic) moralism.

The idea that one can have a revolutionary art without an evolutionary society.

Art as a sanctuary (perhaps the only one) for the individual. The imagination transcendent as it becomes depersonalized, though not yet abstract.

Self-absorption in the grand manner: Elitism.

The ambivalence of a transitional age. Romanticized notion of Classicism.

The simultaneous expression of supreme, even ethereal self-confidence, coextensive with the agony of self-loathing.

The idea of art as an increasingly technical, even scientific process; the autonomy of technique.

The artist both propelled and repelled by vague obligations, exacerbated by the loss of audience, and the potential irrelevance of art.

The task of art, therefore, is its *own* self-realization, outside and beyond the established order.

Wordsworth's injunction to the poet — as Harry Levin puts it — is that he "carry sensation into the midst of the objects of science itself . . . " [the defensive version of which is to preserve and nurture individual consciousness within an increasingly inhuman industrial society]; thus the basic strategic concern of the Modernists was through aesthetics to create a new morality, to "create a conscience for a scientific age." However one might defend Post-Modernism, it cannot be said that it recreates this conscience with much enthusiasm or effect. When consciousness itself is under extreme modification, and when science is generally viewed as dehumanizing, the momentum of knowledge tends to make the moral sense seem a retrograde imperative, associated with discredited realist aesthetics. It is the lack of any moral grounding which makes contemporary work so unpalatable to those who revere the Modernists, and yet their critique, no matter how pretentious or provincial, cannot be finally ignored, much less explained away by art which denies *all* prerogatives as a matter of course. "History," said Zola, "is not a wastebasket." He didn't know the half of it.

2. The Second Revolution

I think this is the great sin of the intellectual: that he never really tests his ideas by what it would mean to him if he were to undergo the experience that he is recommending.

—Lionel Trilling

It is astonishing to observe, in America . . . to what extent the literary atmosphere is a non-conductor of criticism . . .

—Edmund Wilson

The Post-Modernist mentality can only be understood as the product of *two* revolutions. The first revolution is that remarkable explosion of artistic talent and high skepticism, so broadly based yet chronologically concentrated, which wrenched us forever from 19th Century Positivism and whose accomplishments were in place by the First World War. The Second is the revolution in pedagogy and criticism which interpreted, canonized and capitalized the Modernist industry, making "the contemporary" the indubitable cultural reference point. Indeed, we now have a new audience, rather like the 17th century audience for music, which has never been exposed to anything that *isn't* contemporary. But the point is that the Second Revolution, insofar as literature is concerned, is the focus of artistic reaction; the First Revolution comes to us as a reconstituted dream of the Second. Modernism is transmitted through criticism, to the extent that the two revolutions have become indistinguishable.

When we talk about the Modern, we are at this point talking about Interpretation—how literature enters the social context. And authority in criticism is social, not logical. If one wants a real lesson in culture shock, it isn't necessary to reread the Surrealists, but simply compare

the literary curricula of any American university, 1930-45, with those
of the last two decades. Since the Post-Modernist sense of history (when
it exists at all) is almost always truncated between Modernism and
Today, the fact that the Modernist critics originally had a difficult and
in many ways noble battle with the old line philologists and historical
scholars, is largely forgotten. We are invariably dealing with modes
of transmission which date from 1938 at the earliest.*

Post-Modernism does not begin on its own, but when the Modernist
canon is pronounced closed. Hugh Kenner, for one, is not timid about
drawing the line.

> Since Faulkner's death . . . the American novel has been yielding
> to that sense of arbitrariness of language that provided the poets'
> opportunity in the 1920's . . . Certainly, something has altered
> since the 1920's. When the poets took over the terrain of the
> arbitrary, it was never with such lab-coated reasonableness, such
> courteous explanations that if there was no place to go but the
> moon, still it was better than nothing. Transported there, the
> nature of fiction seems to change more disconcertingly than does
> that of poetry. What does the infinite possibility that stretched
> before Williams signify in the imagination of John Barth's "the
> Literature of Exhaustion?" *[A Homemade World]*

"If something has altered since the 1920's," Kenner isn't telling, nor
is it clear how a "sense of arbitrariness" yields "infinite possibility"
for anyone except the explicator; nevertheless, his gut feeling cannot
be easily dismissed.

Post-Modern consciousness, insofar as it can be said to be acute,
is profoundly aware that the *first* revolution is filtered through the
second, and while the activity of interpretation, codification and
certification is routinely scorned, it is nevertheless incorporated with
begrudging *élan* into The Post-Modern aesthetic. History *is* criticism;
it resembles nothing so much as a Final Examination. The essence of
the Post-Modern strategy is to assimilate voraciously (though rarely
systematically) while simultaneously repudiating assimilation. This
creates the illusion of working in a vacuum, which becomes the late
20th century sense of frontier, playing off a grandiose and highly
structured Modernism against a chaotic endless present. It is a reaction
to a history which is "owned" by the Second Revolution.

---

*Hitler invades Poland. Brooks and Warren publish *Understanding Poetry.*

The professionalization of literature has taken many forms, but the Second Revolution is certainly the Age of the Intermediary. Lionel Trilling sensed the contradictions of this position over twenty years ago." . . . Nothing is more characteristic of modern literature than its discovery and canonization of primal, non ethical energies" — and yet at the very moment this literature is introduced and further canonized in the context of Trilling's humanism, he nevertheless realizes that "the young person . . . can never again know the force and terror of what is being communicated to him by the works he is being examined upon." [*Beyond Culture*] It is this tension between the profound anarchism of Avant-Garde Literature and Liberal political and social thought which Trilling confronted throughout his career but never resolved. Why *should* his students have reacted immediately to an experience which for them was already at third remove? As anyone who has had to teach knows full well, the ability to synthesize bad news, to dispassionately and arbitrarily arrange "terror" in a *syllabus* (surely a distinctively American phenomenon) can be far more dispiriting than an Artaud yelling "no more masterpieces!"

Trilling complains of the disappearance of a true "Adversary" culture (he got a third-rate one, briefly, in 1968) and yet he never saw that the entire enterprise of which he is a part has made such a thing irrelevant; the middle class has learned how not to be so middle class, to prefer Kafka to Wouk — at least on Examinations. It is the middle class's historical destiny to have it both ways. (There is of course another intriguing possibility — which does not occur to Trilling or any other theorist of the "free-floating intellectual," and that is that the middle class is shrewder, more resilient, more unified and pragmatically perceptive than the vanguard intellectual; which is why they are the middle class, and why intellectuals, through the university, have made an unspoken alliance with them.)

As for that "Adversary culture" — those hypothetical refugees from the Bourgeoisie whose self-image is one of autonomy and independence yet whose *function* is a mediating one between classes — Gramsci notes, "The mode of the new intellectual can no longer consist in eloquence, which is an exterior and momentary mover of passions, but in active participation in practical life . . . a permanent persuader . . . " [*Prison Notebooks*] Yet, from Carlyle's Hero to the present indefinite, the Humanist intellectual has clearly become one of our least important modern persons, much less a "permanent persuader."

This business of an "Adversary" culture is worth pursuing, for if the contemporary writer often confuses the sensibility of Modernism with the smugness of the Second Revolution, he also confuses the vast plurality of the Bourgeois order with the jurisdiction of commercial institutions. The self-styled Adversary does not foresee the possibility that Bourgeois culture may have escaped Bourgeois control, or that any critique of Bourgeois consciousness must be to some extent self-criticism.

In this context, there is a further difficulty; for if one takes one's Modernism seriously enough to carry its anarcho-radicalism full term, then does it not seriously challenge the traditional view of the hierarchical humanities, and does not the imagination seem anything but liberal? Humanism in such a context becomes merely another stance, concealing an attachment to various class formations, and a wearisome rhetoric no more prescient than the perennial promise to balance the budget. There is no evidence of Professor Trilling ever having been terrorized by Modern Art, and one can understand the suspicion of those whom he chastises for so effortlessly absorbing the radical breaks of Modernism. If Trilling himself does not express discomfort in the presence of a bruising and outrageous work of art, what then could he expect from his students? Here we have another instance in which "The Audience" can give you a pithy paragraph on Einstein's relativistic physics from Modernism's card catalog, but continue to live their daily lives by Newtonian physics. If it took fifty years for the middle class to absorb Modernism, it is testimony to the exponential effect of social inflation that it took it less than half as long to digest and begin to discard Post-Modernism. One could say that a culture which has so effortlessly assimilated the cultural haberdashery of Freud, Marx and Einstein should have no problem with a few literary fireworks; our century has accustomed us to art which takes off like a rocket and comes down like a stick. But the more interesting possibility is that we are dealing with an audience which is more learned and less attentive at the same time, an audience which has been taught how to absorb terror through terminology.

However much Post-Modernism puts itself at odds with the energies of interpretation, it must also promote its own interpretive schema as a way of creating a context for itself — and it is precisely such activity which the culture rewards. The audience no longer asks to be moved, even entertained; but rather to be situated, interpreted, *diagnosed*; an instant mediation which provides a holding action until the next vocabulary gains ascendancy. The rage to be "with it" is not merely the superficial response mocked by "tough-minded" intellectuals; it is often a genuine attempt to find a basis upon which to make judgments, an accommodation with history itself. And it is this very vulnerability which Post-Modernism exploits with gestures of authority offered and taken away simultaneously. Modernism provided its audience an identity by establishing an Olympian if often wrong-headed purity and aplomb against society's generalized corruption and prejudices. Post-Modernism, by undercutting its own authority, initially identifies with its defensive audience, but ultimately chastises it through the self-abnegating refusal to carry through the consequences of its attack. As opposed to the Modernist effect of shocking an audience, the Post-Modernist often seems content to infuriate it by letting everybody off the hook.

> Is it over? Can't you read between the lines?
> One more step. Goodbye suspense. Goodbye.
>
> Blank.
>
> [John Barth, "Title"]

Given Post-Modernism's own central ambivalence and scattershot historical sense, it is not surprising that reactions among more sober critics tend to run the gamut — from Irving Howe who feels that Post-Modernism is some kind of mass culture phenomenon, "impatient with mind," and Harry Levin who finds it "anti-intellectual," to John Gardner who finds it *hyper*-intellectual;

> not very interested in the truth . . . aesthetic game players . . . juggling, obscenely giggling and gesturing in the wings while the play of life goes on . . . *[On Moral Fiction]*

and Robert Alter who is more to the point:

> . . . in this vehemently contemporary fiction, there is a cultivated quality of rapid improvization, often a looseness of form; love of pastiche, parody, slapdash invention; a willful neglect of psychological depth and subtlety or consecutiveness of characterization; a cavalier attitude toward consistency of

incident, plot unity, details of milieu, and underlying all these a
kind of despairing skepticism, often tinged with the exhilaration
of hysteria, about the validity of language and the very enterprise
of fiction. *[Partial Magic]*

And if that seems peremptory, there remains the legitimate question
whether a fully assimilated Modernism can provide *any* continuity. In
Stephen Spender's words:

> The Moderns did not go back into the tradition, they brought
> it forward as an instrument with which to attack the present, i.e.
> there was a way of being traditional which was modern. They did
> so because they felt that the quality of something unprecedented
> about the conditioning of industrial societies somehow altered all
> relations of the individual to his environment. The characteristic
> gesture of modern genius was to produce vast all-inclusive works,
> mansions without foundations. Stein produced her stuttering
> language which was meant to sustain a 'continuous present.' The
> great modern achievements were wagers which made gestures,
> invented methods, *but laid no foundations for a future literature.**
> They led in the direction of an immensity from which there was
> bound to be a turning back because to go further would lead to
> a new and completer fragmentation, utter obscurity, formlessness
> without end. *[The Struggle of the Modern]*

But if a revision of the Modern canon is to be based upon the
recognition of its "daemonic" potential for utter formlessness, it must
always nevertheless contend with the Second Revolution's interest in
making Modernism the reigning cultural orthodoxy. Without this
"managerial revolution," Modernism would not play the major role
in our consciousness that it does. Such interpretive certification becomes
the dominant reality, not that pure terror (or awe) for which Trilling
looked in vain in his students.

It is very tempting to apply the sociological model of *Buddenbrooks*
here. The first generation makes the money; the second achieves social
respectability; the third (you know who) descends into a malaise which
it thinks is aesthetic. The Second Revolution socializes and integrates
art through an inflationary explosion of discourse, generating secular
literary contexts which "look" scientific and philosophical as they once

*Emphasis added.

"looked" historical and religious; secondary languages which, like all 20th century disciplines, try to get behind the subjectivity of human knowledge, guarding the limits of their "scientific" orientation from the consciousness of the world.

This results in a very odd series of relations. Contemporary society is highly fragmented by infinite sub-divisions of groups based on skills, occupation, class, lifestyle, religion, ethnicity and special interests almost too staggering to imagine. Literary art too, in its unprecedented multiplicity of voice, is equally fragmented. But there is no one-to-one or mimetic relationship between the social and literary fragments; they are merely contiguous in some fashion. Add to this a profusion of discourse which also denies any reciprocal relations. The hyper-pluralism of the social order is exceeded only by multiple versions of art, which in turn are exceeded only by the multiplicity of interpretations. As hyper-pluralism destroys the continuity of the legislative process in the political order, so hyper-pluralism in art and criticism destroys the possibility of eponymy. In such a situation the contemporary consumer of art is in the position of the Weimar burgher who paid for his dinner *before* he ate it, as there was no telling how it would be revalued if he waited until he was finished to see how he liked it.

The Second Revolution cannot be understood only in terms of a simple reduction of a first enthusiasm to the routine, or the charismatic to the institutional. Modern criticism, for all its elitist tone, represents *in toto* a democratization of access to the literary world, making its own market through pedagogy and by presumably exemplifying extra-literary values which were once thought of as civilizing. If the thrust of Modern art is towards formlessness, then the thrust of Modern criticism is towards formal gestures of autonomy without content.

Yet hyper-pluralism qualifies the very existence of extra-literary values as interpretation seems to become an almost accidental response to literature. In Roland Barthes's hyperbole, contrary to creating something original, ". . . writing is the destruction of every voice, every point of view; literature is a multidimensional space in which a variety of writings, none of them original, blend and crash . . . " This dissipates any creative tension which might naturally grow out of a true adversary relation.

For the lay observer, in this case both the reader and the "creative writer," the final verdict on the Second Revolution is that it does not aim for a stable culture at all, but revels in the stock market of vocabularies of self-description, in the mutually exclusive methods and half-lived ideas, indistinguishable in their velocity from those of the commercial world which functions as a unifying scapegoat. The Second Revolution comes to exemplify a profusion of methodologies without a *methodenstreit* (a conflict of rival methodologies). Not only are all methods and subject matters incorporated into the acquisitions program of the Humanities, but once the market for criticism is saturated, "creative" writing is also absorbed into the Pantheon, and by opening new jobs, if not careers, avoids what would have provoked in almost any other culture a contest between opposed disciplines, if not ideologies. In such a vacuum, the triumph of Modernist orthodoxy is complete — to use *Time* magazine's words, "Modernism *is* our institutional culture!" The critical establishment neither usurps nor reasserts authority — it simply trades off intellectual hierarchy while retaining institutional tenure, defaulting like the good manager with his golden parachute, while retaining the smugness of privileged access. This is what Adorno called 'progressive half-culture', "invented for those who feel that they have been judged by history, or at least that they are falling, but who still strut in front of their peers as if they were an interior elite." *[The Jargon of Authenticity]*

"This second (literary) environment," Trilling tells us, astonishingly enough, "must always have some ethical and spiritual advantage over the first (the general culture of reality) if only because, even though its influence and its personnel grow apace, it will never have actual rule of the world." *[Beyond Culture]*

In the Second Revolution, criticism forfeits its Adversary role by denying that it is fundamentally rooted in the Bourgeois being it pretends to criticize; on the other hand, it forfeits its Conservatory role by refusing to confront the false homogeneity and devalued standards within its own congery of disciplines. The Second Revolution makes all art potentially respectable and accessible by making literary criticism a primary *appanage* of the middle class. The Post-Modern era is given both its energizing and enervating force by the *inflation of discourse*, a market which does not reach equilibrium, but only that satiety common to all systems clogged with transactions, leaving all major questions unresolved.

It is the poignant and central confusion of the Post-Modern writer that he rarely gets down to seriously questioning the assumptions of the First Revolution, but relieves his frustration and conceals his hopes in his antipathy to the Second — which, ironically enough, represents his only potential audience. And it is this context of continual non-confrontation and nonjudgmentalism which provides contemporary literary culture with its predictability and its sense of sour irrelevance.

3. Exploiting the Dead Issue

I recognized something more than the melancholy of a lost cause.
The whole infelicity speaks of a cause that could never have been
gained.

—*Henry James,* The American Scene

We have become used to terms being beaten into blankness — but
what do we do with a term that never had any meaning to begin with?
Labels for the ongoing are invariably sloppy, which is one reason most
critics sensibly eschew the present entirely. In the efforts to propound
a Post-Modernism, there is an air of melodrama which suggests either
that something is happening far beyond the establishment's powers to
recognize it, or that nothing of moment is occurring — which is all the
more terrifying.

Note that we have not as yet mentioned a single specific author, yet
already there are attitudes, antipathies, historical views and even
aesthetic choices which are marshalled on behalf of this black hole in
the present. We are dealing with a particularly sensitive and elusive
Geist, a cluster of dead ends which are nevertheless accumulatively
pertinent.

To take one example, some fourteen years ago John Barth wrote a
modest essay, essentially an homage to Borges, in which he used the
phrase, "The Literature of Exhaustion," echoing George Kubler's
mechanistic notion that "every new form limits the succeeding
innovations in the same series." Whether this is at all true in a medium
as plasmatic as literature, and even if it is true, whether it is a good
idea to take as a basis for one's own work, is not the point here. The
term has certainly haunted Barth, and he has recently chosen to
elaborate it in a sequel essay, yet another echo of Fry's *"pushing things
a little further. . . ."* What Barth wants now for literature is *"the next*

best thing . . . what I hope might be thought of one day as a literature of replenishment . . . '', which seems an altogether reasonable if not very helpful or ambitious program, the sort that George Babbitt would not have found unpalatable.

Exactly what was enfeebled fourteen years ago, and where we are now to discover our provender is not a question which has been pursued very diligently, despite the fact that the initial essay was treated (unfairly in retrospect) as a kind of benchmark in some larger reorganization of strategies. This remains an astonishing instance of a nice occasional piece, seized upon in a cultural vacuum, and bloated by repeated reference into a fake orismology.

Robert Scholes, in reviewing *Giles Goat-Boy*, betrays the exegetical motive here. "For some time, we have been *wondering what to do with the training** given to us by those giants of Modern fiction, whether we were really meant to expend our hard earned responsiveness on such estimable but unexciting writers as C.P. Snow and Saul Bellow." This "hard earned training" continues to erect charters for contemporary writing with little success. If there is any common ground among contemporary fiction writers at all, it is their uneasiness, as heirs to the Second Revolution, at being explained in terms of yet another movement. There is very little in existing critical categories which might help us to understand living writers as historical men and women. Rather, we still have a landscape populated by Wastelanders, Absurdists, Black Humorists, Fabulists, *et alia*.

But if one does take Barth's argument seriously, then why did no one bother to apply a bit of common sense to it? Perhaps because institutional Modernism had to be deconstructed by any means available? The proclamation that "it's all been done" certainly demands some circumspect ridicule. But the basic idea which underlies both of Barth's essays is a profoundly unexamined one. When he says, "There's no going back to Tolstoy and Dickens & Co.," he is saying essentially that because of what we've become in the 20th century, both as artists and people, we cannot go back to the past — particularly a past in which writers commanded a central respect in the culture. But these are two very different questions, and we ought not confuse holistic cultural assertions with literary strategies. "The worst and most corrupting lies," says Bernanos, "are problems wrongly stated." Just what is it about the 20th century experience which makes us so unable

*Emphasis added.

to utilize the past? The Modernists, for all their obsessive up-to-dateness, certainly had no reluctance to going back to make it new. If Barth himself can "go back" to Smollett and Defoe and Fielding, then why not to Tolstoy and Dickens? Is it that you cannot recapture authority or sensibility but only form? Or that the 18th century is more assimilable for us than the 19th? It would seem that we are cut off only from *preselected* portions of the past, and rather than idealize a period of history as traditional movements have done, we can only up the amnesiac's ante.

Modernism is a ditch which we must crawl through or leap over to experience the history which is also ours. Post-Modernism is a period characterized by an absolute failure of theory, a plethora of dead issues — which is not to say a dead issue cannot be exploited. What Barth seems to be insisting upon is that the only way to come to terms with the discrepancy between Art and the Real Thing is to affirm the artificial element in art, make it part of the work, as there is no getting rid of it in any case. But the absence of coherent theory is not as significant as is the willed absence of any historical sense, save an ambivalent antipathy to the "owned history" of the Second Revolution. History becomes merely the history of artifice. The only usable past is aesthetics.

Nevertheless, the *absence* of history conceals its own historical theory, both aesthetic and cultural, a theory which resists stasis on principle, and views progress (or entropy) in art as utterly linear. Exhaustion as a theory is just as unitary in its way as was 19th century realism, in which art was a steady accumulator rather than a divestor of experience.

Slipshod theory, it must be said, doesn't seem to have made much of a difference in the quality or variety of American fiction during its contemporary ascendancy. The American prose novel, after all, is one of our few national aesthetic projects which can make exhilarating claims within an international context. Dead issues are not necessarily dead ends. How long fiction can continue to exploit its abandonment of historical sense, and perhaps more importantly, the absence of a coherent constituency, is the more interesting question. It may very well be that we have entered a period in which literature will stubbornly persist without either internal coherence or enthusiastic response. It would not be the first time. Indeed, it is preeminently in the Modernist period that the European sense of recreant and reciprocal culture was felt to be within our grasp, which accounts for the peculiar combination of nostalgia and embitterment which Americans reserve for the recent past.

"Can't go backness" is its own theory and as such provides whatever intellectual currency literature has at present. But liberation from history exacts its own boredom and determinism. It exaggerates antecedents only as obstacles. It apportions historical experience without any principle of selection, and aestheticizes experience without question. While mimicking philosophy rather than history, it nevertheless sidesteps the question of origins, which is to say, it refuses to take final responsibility for its own strategies, and formalizes desperation as a virtue of necessity.

The "historical sense" is not slavishly reverent of the past, nor is it necessarily associated with a return to Realism. It emphasizes only that absurdity is an historical and not an ontological condition, and thus grants a perspective to the appropriateness of techniques which trade off total self-absorption, the tendency of internal analysis to rush in where social consciousness is weak.

The 19th century was the first century without an identifiable period style and a single repertory of opinions. Modernism was the first period which did not predicate a state by which it could be judged complete. And Post-Modernism is the first period which does not idealize some specific historical period as an emulative model, or attempt to recapture the purity, however illusory, of some vanished age.

4. The Threnody of Solipsism

*I am weary of my individuality and simply nauseated by other
people's.*

—*D.H. Lawrence*

Those who take up the notion that Post-Modernist art has suddenly
become self-referential commit the grossest ahistoricism, and confuse
whatever claims might be made on behalf of the present. Clearly, the
inward seeking motif is not only fully exploited in works as early and
obvious as *Tristram Shandy* or *Jacques the Fatalist*, but also crops up
continually where one wouldn't expect it. Even in literatures as naive
as, say, Rumanian fairy tales, one frequently senses an active
impatience with the arbitrariness of narrative conventions.

> Once upon a time something happened. If it had not happened,
> it would not be told . . . when the girl reached her sixteenth year,
> the same thing befell her that happens to all beautiful maidens —
> a dragon came, stole her, and carried her far away . . . we won't
> linger over the story any longer, we know what always happens
> when dragons and princes meet . . .

[*"The Poor Boy,"* circa 1885]

More importantly, as Erich Kahler, among others, shows
conclusively, the internalization of narrative is part of a general inward
movement of human consciousness as a whole. "Consciousness expands
as man constantly redraws outer space, the contents of a more and more
complex world, into what Rilke called *Weltinnenraum*, 'World inner
space.' " *[The Inward Turn of Narrative]* What Kahler demonstrates
is that in one important sense the entire course of history has been
advancing to the self-consciousness of the actual, which tradition had

previously accepted only as a philosophical postulate. The internalization of narrative is the movement from external action and epic adventure to the ever deeper and more intense exploration of character and personality.

Post-Modernism can hardly be defined as unique in its self-consciousness. There is, of course, the "I can't go on, I'll go on" school, and Beckett has certainly taken this notion as far as it can go in any sustainable narrative; whether he is the last of the Modernists or the first of the Post-Modernists is a question of a low order of importance. Rather what is distinguishing about Post-Modernist self-consciousness is its *aggressiveness*; the dynamic in which the author both involves and skeptifies the reader — almost as if the reader were not really there — *evoking the audience as cultural enemy*. There is no "Ah, gentle reader," but rather: "now that I've got you alone down here you bastard don't think I'm letting you get away easily, no sir, not you brother; anyway, how do you think you are going to get out, down here where it is dark and oily like an alley, meaningless as Plato's cave? Do you think you know the way? Well, you don't know anything, do you?" [William Gass, *Willie Masters' Lonesome Wife*]

We are dealing here with what might be called a heightened sense of the unreality of the audience, which is more than a philosophical problem. In Nabokov and Borges, for example, there is acute self-consciousness, unambiguous *dédoublement*, an awareness that the cultural transaction itself may be snatched away by historical catastrophe at any moment, and that at best the audience mistranslates everything. Yet at the same time there remains the belief that history is audience. To believe in the possibility of creative imagination is to presuppose an audience which not only changes, but *can* be changed. If reality is unalterable, then human activity, much less literature, is robbed of meaning. For all their old world elitism, these writers never treat their readers as roughly or contemptuously as our contemporaries. One must obviously believe in potential reciprocity before one can afford to be manipulative, and in this sense, Nabokov and Borges are *pre*-Modernist.

The involution of Post-Modern consciousness does not concern the psychological Self so much as the increasingly problematic relationship between the writer and the reader. Of all the structural certitudes which purport to explain human behavior, psychology has certainly suffered more than any. The Humanist notion that you must go to literature for any detailed understanding of human character has been essentially discarded in Post-Modern writing. The attitude often seems to be 'what you see is what you get.' Barthelme questions whether 'the Figure in the Carpet,' "is just . . . carpet." The attack on the very idea of *explicable* motivation does not necessarily demean the complexity of human nature, but rather the easy reductions of the psychoanalytic system which gives a predetermined shape to personality and action. Such recalcitrance nevertheless plays hell with any traditional notion of plot, to the extent that *all* cause and effect is intrinsically suspicious. But if we adopt Kahler's formulation, Post-Modern self-consciousness aborts the progressively intense exploration of "character and personality" which is the *sine qua non* of Humanist psychology. Ahistoricism reveals itself in contemporary literary strategy as, above all, anti-psychological. Post-Modernist literature attacks cause and effect in psychology just as surely as Einstein attacked the concept of before and after in nature.

On the face of it, metaphors of "usedupness" and randomness are not only convenient ways of challenging what remains of conventional notions of progress and linearity, but also remind us that while movements, nations, and cultures get used up with increasing regularity, there remains a striking continuity in the persistent and endless verbal innovation of man. What is striking, in fact, is precisely the opposite of Barth's notion of hapless finitude, namely, the astonishing durability and inexhaustibility of literature as its own institution. What we are experiencing in Post-Modern involution is the private mind asserting itself, not against a well-organized conspiracy of taste, nor totalitarian propaganda, but against what it perceives as an increasingly homogenized, passive and inaccessible public mind. The intensity of this self-assertion *is* something new; its querulousness goes far beyond the necessity of reacting against the falsity of antecedent literature. Its aggressivity employs self-doubt as a means of arousing interest, if not precisely sympathy. This is a Narcissism mobilized at a new level of defensive rather than celebratory expression, in which the object (audience) is blamed in advance for a failure in communication. It recalls those ritualistic dedications of the minor 16th century nobility whose authors often prefaced their treatises by humbling themselves before the *symbol* of their audience, offering a "poor book" against the vast knowledge of the "Lord" even as it became thoroughly clear as the text progressed that the writer regarded the object of his dedication as a craven idiot.

It was Modernism's obligation to distinguish between conventional entertainment and art which challenged social and cultural norms. With Post-Modernism, the euphemisms of 'entertainment' and 'seriousness' are at categorical odds with one another. Against a hedonistic adolescent culture, Post-Modernism erects an ideolocracy of discomfiture, in which irony functions as the intellectual's only sentiment.

It is a strange world, at any rate, when confessional autobiography is considered "realistic" rather than self-indulgent, while if a narrator lets us on to the fact that it *is* a story he is telling, then he is "self-conscious." What is more interesting to note is that in any conventional catalogue of our contemporaries, you will find out practically nothing about the writers as "selves." The writer as public megalomaniac is no longer in vogue. Television is not kind to the literary personality. And there is the further presumption that the revealed self is toxic to the imagination, that the compositional self is the only real being.

While this represents an altogether admirable and understandable attempt to eliminate the celebrity function from writing, it does eventually delimit possibilities and acquires its own monotony, just as surely as Hemingway's or Mailer's bald self-promotion limited the risks they might take aesthetically and finally destroyed their work. Instead of open self-aggrandizement, we now get tongue-in-cheek statements about the forfeiture of pleasure which aesthetic retooling necessitates.

Increasingly, throughout the century, our interiority, once thought to be a precious legacy, is seen as a curse until we arrive at a post-historical consciousness which is defined only by the reverberations of the *next* present. Experience is seen either as a new movement or out of date; both the ongoing moment *and* any sense of continuity suffer dramatically. It is not surprising that we have a literature with no characters, only situations.

This suggests two things. First, that we have idealized or immemorialized the immediate past — Modernism — and second, that if an artist is to deal with what he perceives to be his historical inferiority, he has other options than inferiorizing his own work. One of the faults of our age is to be emblematic of a situation rather than descriptive of it.

By dismissing self-consciousness as the bench mark of the present, we can move on to question whether in fact we are distinguished by anything, save for an ambivalent reaction to high Modernism. But one thing ought to be clear by now. The new literary aggressivity assaults not only the reader's bourgeois moralism, his bourgeois notions of entertainment and instruction, but his very *place* in the literary transaction. The author has not only exposed the shape of the reader's illusion, forsaken the olympian omniscient stance of the High Modernist, but has become, through aggressive indifference to conventional psychology, interlocutor, intermediary, and auditor. This incessant shifting of authority is not merely an aesthetic choice, but reflects a deeply embedded uneasiness permeating all literary affairs.

What is most indicative of Post-Modern self-consciousness is the extent to which it eschews the psychological for the compositional self. And coextensively, the only tendency all Post-Modern arts hold in common is the sense, as a post-historical enterprise, that art is a commentary on the aesthetic history of whatever genre it adopts.

Self-reflexivity is nothing new, and in any case does not hold within itself a new image of man. It is nothing more or less than another subordinated technique. The journey into the interior is not quite the assembly line we have made it.

5. The Sublation of the Avant-Garde

I can truly say that I am not in the world, and this is not a mere mental attitude . . . I prefer to show myself as I am, in my inexistence and uprootedness . . . but, the reader must believe that it is a matter of an actual sickness *and not a phenomenon of the age, of a sickness which is related to the essence of the human being and his central possibility of expression . . .*

—*Antonin Artaud*

To use the term with any historical precision (that is, to use European literary movements as some kind of analogue for American literary experience) we can only conclude that there never existed a genuine Avant-Garde in this country, and if one wishes to study a continuing Avant-Garde at the present time, one must look to a few totalitarian societies. The Avant-Garde defines itself historically by the rigidity of the official culture to which it opposes itself, *tout court*. Where rigidity does not exist, it is hypothesized so that attacks upon it can be vindicated.

If our self-consciousness is less comprehensive than it appears, the orthodoxy of the Avant-Garde posture also requires some circumspection. To throw off the provincialism of a William Dean Howells, for example, or to start *Poetry* Magazine by soliciting door-to-door — these are not inconsiderable achievements. But to compare the indifference of Chicago entrepreneurs to the total control of European Academic Classicism is to miss the point: that the European Avant-Garde consisted of extremely well-organized and well-funded movements, politicized parties more coherent than many of the "real" political parties in their national parliaments. Where else but in Secessionist Vienna could one find the Avant-Garde building a museum for itself?

In retrospect, it would seem that the systematic destruction of European Humanism by the so-called Modern Revolution in its most profound and catastrophic form was simply incomprehensible to the American emigrés, for whom it was yet another revolution perceived from a sidewalk cafe. Even remarkable figures like Pound or Eliot seemed to have a genius for latching on to the most peripheral figures of the European movements, not to mention their aberrant politics.

It cannot be emphasized enough that the Avant-Garde was for Europe a profoundly cultural and political revolution, while for America, from the very first, it was essentially an *aesthetic* movement — a technical reform of syntax, vocabulary, and tone — and so it remains. Post-Modernism's stylistic innovations at their best are not mere imitations of the Avant-Garde, but they nevertheless remained rooted in a critique of culture so fully assimilated that it can no longer claim any adversary moral or political authority. In fact, Post-Modernism's best satirical energies have been directed at the programmatic agonism of the Avant-Garde, the romantic belief that the artist can only fulfill his function by positioning himself well outside the culture. The most heartbreaking but instructive aspect of Post-Modernism is, indeed, the attempt of the literary artist to fight his way back into the culture.

That many of our best writers go unread does not put them ahead of their time. "Suffering does not ennoble," as Somerset Maugham says, "it embitters." So while we have had communities in some sense — the group of New York intellectuals and their largely honorable battle to keep democratic socialist ideas alive, for example — the very idea of a true adversary community with a coherent, even consensual, point of view (*much less* an establishment whose taste is not only a foregone conclusion but which manifests and enforces its own standards) is pure myth.

Culturally Conservative critics (Rosenberg, Kramer, Howe, *et al.*) have attacked such pretenses brilliantly, but even in their fury, there remains a nostalgia for a community in which artists and intellectuals might share something beyond an antipathy to Richard Nixon. Their analysis falls short precisely in not recognizing that the Avant-Garde is compromised not so much by Bourgeois acceptance *as by absorption into the intelligentsia* — at a time when the artist requires *publicity* more than direct financial patronage.

For these critics, the very idea of Post-Modernism muddles an already confused situation, and they are undoubtedly right. To be a cultural conservative in this day and age is to puncture grandiosity, and avoid making a fool of oneself, but it is also to ignore the confusing multiplicity of experience, which though it may be currently overrated, is nevertheless a fact of contemporary life — one which no judgmentalism, however shrewd, can adequately convey.

Nevertheless, the suspicion that our social and artistic inflation is incapable of producing the kind of high art which we associate historically with the single-minded has a nagging legitimacy. How such art could be recognized, if in fact it was produced in such diversity, is an even more interesting question — and the conservatives' argument is invariably weakened by their definition of culture as something which has failed *them*. For all its pertinacious and appropriate ridicule of the American Avant-Garde, the conservative critique is still grounded in a theory of Art in which a culture-bearing class confers distinctions and sets norms, a critique which is finally a lament for the conservatives' own waning influence. Conservative intellectuals remain the only fraction of the middle class which identifies its own survival with the survival of high culture, which in this case is Modernism, and their pessimism is conditioned by the fact that the culture is no longer in their control.

Or to put it another way: in the context of proliferating subcultures it is extremely difficult to gain an identity as a summarizer or overseer of culture. As the analect's professional concerns become more specialized, the more generalized and vague his theory of culture becomes. What we get are significant changes of style within subcultures, which signal *nothing* about a change in the larger culture. In effect we are dealing with a new Regionalism whose definition is not geographical but aesthetic (and regionalism is the most scorned of the older notions of criticism). We invariably cast aspersions on an age which cannot be defined by a great mind, a mind which can at least exemplify the larger pattern. The critics' job is made immeasurably more difficult by the lack of truly authoritative figures. In fact, we cannot imagine an age which has some merit but no distinguishing monuments of mind.

Moreover, we have no adequate theory to explain the *indifference* of market economics; the artists' lot can hardly be characterized as the result of a conspiracy in any conventional sense of the word. Despite the most pointed of attacks ["paranoia resolves," Freud said, in an ultimate instance of 19th century optimism] the only thing that can be said against the publishing establishment is that it is basically timid, quick to exploit fashion, and averse to losing money. No heroes or real villains there. Since it is grandly assimilative like the upper middle class which staffs it, it really has no identifiable taste and therefore cannot operate authoritatively. Pervasiveness is not authority; the power of market share is essentially *displacement*, a new kind of power, the power of oligopoly by default, and vague Marxist sentiments will provide no analysis here. To quote an editor in a New York trade house, "we are too ignorant for anything to happen to us on a high plane of degeneracy." In our time, it is petty venality and mushheadedness, not tyranny, which characterize high capitalist bottomline authority. Ortega reminds us that mass-man flourishes as profusely among the upper classes as the proletariat. He rarely presents himself as a conventional adversary. He has read his Nietzsche and knows that no truth shall bind him.

The fact remains that no Avant-Garde can exist when the Establishment is not coherent enough to attack. If there is an American Avant-Garde it can only be described as an overlapping succession of an historically unprecedented *number* of Avant-Gardes, none of which has captured an enduring authority.

We should not be surprised that the Avant-Garde has ended up where it has, i.e., everywhere. As Renato Poggioli points out:

> In a democratic society, the tyranny of opinion easily dominates in moral as in cultural matters; but such tyranny is incapable of exercising decisive sanctions and establishing absolute conformity. That society ends up by tolerating, in a limited but not restricted sphere of action, displays of eccentricity and non-conformity, tolerating individuals and groups who transgress rather than follow the norm. In the cultural field, too, democratic society is therefore forced to admit, beyond the official and normative art, precisely that other art which has been called, as a synonym for avant-garde art, the art of exception. Avant-garde art cannot help paying involuntary homage to democratic and liberal-bourgeois society in the very act of proclaiming itself antidemocratic and antibourgeois; nor does it realize that it expresses the evolutionary and progressive principle of that social order in the very act of abandoning itself to the opposite chimeras of involution and revolution . . . *[The Theory of the Avant Garde]*

Ours is certainly not a time of rest and recreation, nor does it seem to be a period of consolidation, lacking as it does a great master to give it tone or label. In some sense, Post-Modernism is a holding action, a mood which appropriates all the stale metaphors of transition while gripped in the fear of stasis. To reverse Beckett's infamous dictum: 'the noise of emptiness in the frolic of revolt.' The Avant-Garde is now decay when it is not imitative nostalgia. In such a situation we ought to resist the atmosphere of manufactured crisis which is nothing but pluralism as evasion.

The most damaging hangover of Avant-Garde pretensions remains the concept of technical breakthrough, of art as the experimental adjunct of scientific methodology, to the demands of which it does not submit — experiment as bluff. The truly experimental novel exists only in the mind of critics. Hans Magnus Enzensberger writes:

> The historic avant-garde perished by its aporias. It was questionable, but it was not craven. Never did it try to play it safe with the excuse that what it was doing was nothing more than an 'experiment'; it never cloaked itself in science in order to be absolved of its results. That distinguishes it from the company of limited responsibility that is its successor; therein lies its greatness. . . . The path of modern arts is not reversible. Let others harbor hopes for the end of modernity, for conversions and 'reintegrations.' What is to be chalked up against today's avant-garde is not that it has gone too far but that it keeps the back doors open for itself, that it seeks support in doctrines and collectives, and that it does not become aware of its own aporias, long since disposed of by history. It deals in a future that does not belong to it. Its movement is regression. The avant-garde has become its opposite: anachronism. That inconspicuous, limitless risk, in which the artists' future lives — it cannot sustain it . . . with the designation *experiment*, the avant-garde excuses its results, takes back, as it were, its "actions", and unloads all responsibility on the receiver . . . *[Die Aporien du Avantgarde]*

The fact of the matter is that no one knows what it means to be *Avant-Garde* these days, aside from a certain dress or peremptory manner. From a sociological point of view there are indeed two *distributive* cultures, and they can hardly be reduced to a conflict between Science and Humanism. One culture is the conventional communications industry, increasingly an adjunct of the kinetic media, a planetary system of increasingly mergered bodies which conform to an increasingly inexorable set of mundane laws. This culture is

surrounded by a secondary culture of little magazines, subsidized
journals, university animadversions, a constellation of infinite but
mostly hapless energy which, when viewed from the planets, has no
apparent force of its own, each particle from the distance emitting the
same equivalent light, and from which issues from time to time a
shooting star.

The rigid compartmentalization of these two systems has no European
counterpart and is totally without historical precedent. This is what
happens when the diversity and incessant innovation celebrated by
Modernism loses its elitist thrust, its minority exclusivity, its dialectical
relation with the official culture, and becomes democratized, socially
inflated, and spread randomly over a heterogeneous landscape. It defies
conventional historical analysis, for as economic and commercial forces
become more and more concentrated, it seems adversary ideology and
style become even more fragmented. We don't even know whether this
amounts to radical eclecticism *or* pluralism — whether we are dealing
with a number of independent realities or arbitrary competing systems.
These are the contradictions we should dwell upon, rather than trying
to resurrect the dissipated scandal of Modernism in which a band of
outsiders storm the Temple, like a film run backwards to puerile
laughter. We will never again have a figure like Pound, because the
culture is simply not manipulable by even the most consummate literary
tactician.

One suspects that energy expended upon attacking an audience which
does not exist and an establishment which will not acknowledge itself
is as misspent as that expended on pandering to the lowest common
denominator. It is this innocent fact, of a *real* non-existent audience
and a *genuine* indifference to Art, which the Post-Modern artist
confronts if not always honestly, at least consciously. To maintain the
militant posture of a Modernistic rebel is not only historically perverse
but refuses contemporary experience. We are not, unfortunately
perhaps, simply the sum total of Western European ways. Nor have
we defined our exceptionality with much precision.

If a "post-industrial" society, as Daniel Bell defines it, is an
"information society" — even one of "alternative" information —it
is a rule of life that such information will tend to become equivalent
and undifferentiated, except insofar as it is given marketing labels,
whether intellectual or commercial. J.H. Huizinga made a precise stab
at this fact when he noted that:

All art is a striving and our over conscious age demands that such striving be given a name . . . art is far more susceptible to mechanization and fashion than science . . . in scientific thinking the -*ism* terms are chiefly limited to the domain of philosophy. Monism, vitalism, idealism are terms indicating a general point of view . . . only when it comes to the philosophical reduction of knowledge to a universal principle do the -*isms* play their part . . . It is a pre-eminently modern phenomenon that art begins with proclaiming a movement which it christens with an -*ism*, and only then attempts to make the corresponding work of art . . . *[In the Shadow of Tomorrow]*

But Huizinga's analysis is perhaps too logical. For as we have seen with Fry's coinage, and in a more minor way with Barth's, terminology may not in fact be generative — even though it alludes to a future that no one knows, least of all the few who may be there. The -*isms* of the present day can be best understood as *a posteriori* theories of structural change which are *neither* myth nor history, but fictions in the most disparaging sense — the writer alluding to what he *might* have done.

If the traditional Avant-Garde was characterized by incessant innovation and the forced consumption of cultural goods, then a good case can be made for capitalist consumer culture as the Avant-Garde of our time. As Gerald Graff puts it, "advanced capitalism needs to destroy all vestiges of tradition, all orthodox ideologies, all continuous and stable forms of reality in order to stimulate higher levels of consumption." Crisis becomes not a revolutionary but the ultimate capitalist metaphor. The American Avant-Garde never confronted the dominant cultural and political institutions of its society. Its linguistic transformations are nothing to be sneezed at, but its orientation would play too easily into the hands of a new linguistic determinism, and, as we shall see, made it that much easier for its attitudes to be integrated into both mass culture and literary theory.

The idea of being willingly cut off from History by aesthetics *is* a distinctly new idea, and one which was Western European before it was American; but only America found the idea, on the whole, salutary. In our recent desuetude, however, we note an increasing weariness with the warlike atonalities and radical confrontation which are the legacy of a European consciousness which was genuinely embattled and whose enemies were obvious and omnipresent. Abstract art, in this sense, was an attack upon the cultural arrogance of the state, and aestheticism was its vanguard. Post-Modernism becomes most confused when it invokes the spectre of a new Totalitarianism as its justification. Consumer capitalism may be a juggernaut, but it is hardly monolithic. We have enormous nostalgia for centralized chauvinistic authority because historically it is easier to identify and thus easier to overthrow.

European Modernism and its Avant-Garde was initially a profoundly social and political movement, while America placed an exclusive emphasis on the aesthetics of Modernism. This is why any attempt to see our literary movements as revolutionary always seems overwrought, just as our few attempts at radical political reform seem so hopelessly literary. The missing social and political ingredient of American Modernism, and it was missing from the first, cannot be overemphasized.

If we miss the point that self-consciousness is simply one subordinated technique among others, we tend also to refuse to see the Avant-Garde as one of many traditions, a tradition which requires a specifically defined adversary. True experimentation uses tradition ruthlessly; it does not expend its major energies in making the past appear old. We live with the knowledge that we are not nearly as advanced as our vitalistic predecessors predicted we would be. It is only recently that we have come to terms with that fact, and have seen our adjustment as having some merit, not simply as another occasion for ritual self-abnegation. The American audience has developed an unbridled affection for the artist who is dumb, self-destructive, isolated and basically crazy. The "Avant-Garde" now deserves the horns of its quotation marks just as much as the "Bourgeois reality" it presumably subverts.

The Avant-Garde, in fact, has become nothing more or less than bourgeois self-criticism.

6. Speculations in Lieu of a Transition

> *. . . while the universal characteristics of the new consciousness, such as self-reference, mind-space and narratization, can develop swiftly on the heels of a new language construction, the larger contours of civilization, the huge landscape of culture against which this happens, can only change with geologic slowness.*
>
> —*Julian Jaynes*

If Modernism attempted to recapture in the world of art the traditional coherences once associated with religion and social order, then is it not perfectly logical for Post-Modernism to challenge and even ridicule this last gasp of Absolutism (and Absolution), to lay bare the means of attaining such a "transcendent" position, and to involve the reader not as an acolyte, but as an accomplice, willing or not, in the destruction of this most complex and perdurable of all illusions? Art can no longer be a sanctuary, when questioning the "classic" formulations of art is central to the artistic transaction. And art as sanctuary is really quite a minor idea, possible only in a period of extreme pessimism and disruption.

Every writer insists that the imagination is the writer's source of authority, that he was not put on the earth to deal with a reality which is already complete. Moreover, even those with no imagination know that the imagination does not operate in a sensory vacuum. Yet the fashionable illusion is that the imagination is validated to the extent to which it eschews external evidence. This is a contradiction very much worth pursuing, because confronting it makes it possible to distinguish between substantial and trivial forms of the imagination, between vision and lies. It is after all the Modernists' high seriousness of purpose, the pretension of art as a sanctuary (when the evidence suggests that it can be clearly a maze, a prison, a battlefield, a gladiola, or anything else one wants to make of it), the grandiose religiosity of art as the *last remaining refuge*, which is so witheringly indicted by Post-modern self-reflexive work.

We should bear in mind that the privileged notion of art as the energizer of discourse still holds — only that art is now seen as a destroyer, not an incidence of sublime power, nullifying the established reality even as it depicts it. To understand this voluntary aspect of literature is absolutely crucial. It is not transcendence which differentiates art from science; it is the very *lack* of external compulsion and absolute imperative which effects its internal dynamics. The creative impulse of modern art is centered in the will, and it is ruminative willfulness precisely which is both the catalyst and catalepsy of the Post-modern temper.

In such a situation even despair no longer has the lofty ring of certainty; true despair, like true cheerfulness, becomes finally untenable, an overrated purgative, too lofty for the skeptical personality. Apocalyptic posturing tends only to make despair abstract and finally unconvincing; its old bittersweet quality becomes manic and obtrusive. When Hemingway's Frederick Henry walks out of the hotel into the rain after losing his lover and child, the peremptory flatness of the ending is meant to counter the melodramatic and sentimental Victorian convention. This kind of silent stoic forbearance tends to crumble under Post-modern levity; it is the single impossible reaction for the Post-modern protagonist. Terminal melancholy is too absolute and high-minded to be sustainable. Even silence is robbed of utter despondency and reified. Melancholy is permitted, as long as it too is leavened with irony. Irony is to the contemporary intellectual what self-absolution is to the modern politician. It certifies a certain necessary seriousness of purpose; it implies secret knowledge which cannot be made entirely public for everyone's good; it forms a reality principle unto itself, the verbal animal's deflection not of alienation but of the terrible straightforward. Irony is no longer a dynamic principle, but the inert substance of the matter. One becomes ironic about irony—infinite reduction becomes the engine of narrative momentum.

Just how commonplace the concept of irony has become can be seen in Brooks and Warren's "Letter to the Teacher" in 1959:

> . . . one of the objections which may be brought against the emphasis on irony [is that] it ends in the celebration of a smug and futile skepticism which is at variance with actual effort which

most successful literary compositions [sic] leave upon the reader. [We] would not endorse any irony which preceded resolution but would endorse an irony which forced the resolution to take stock of as full a context as possible.

How ironical that irony is seen as something which is "endorsable," or that it requires a "full context." We have not had a full context in some time, and the most insulting thing one can now say about another's intelligence is that it is not sufficiently ironical. Post-Modern irony "precedes resolution" by a very large measure indeed.

This is the elitism of the isolated, a cranky elitism because there is no other choice: Flaubert's ambivalence escalated to a mean pitch where supreme self-confidence and self-loathing become self-cancelling. Elitism cannot function as mere aloofness and usually requires more than a coterie to find expression. Elitism is a natural and visceral response to Mass Culture, and as such requires no particular value system. Elitism requires a community, and in retrospect it seems that Modernism, despite the nostalgia of European cafe society, was quite chaotic, when compared to the communities created by the Second Revolution in America, where, enforced by teaching and interpretation, a professional class takes up worrying the notion of literature's relationship to society. Coherence, then, is not imposed by standards, but by curricula. We should never forget that "literature acquires whatever theoretical order it has as a school subject." (Claudio Guillén)

Is it so difficult to understand our obsession with culmination, with self-parody, with the metaphors of exhaustion, with what can be called the *rhetoric of terminality*? The mythology of the Transitional Age takes on an intense, almost baffling quality. If there was ever a national mythology of history, the Transitional Age is America's. Recall that every American generation of the 20th century has described itself by its peculiar myth of deprivation — depression, ennui, repression, the god that failed, nada, darkness at noon, the shining palace built upon the sand, silence, apathy, involution, apocalypse, entropy — the catalogue is as endless as it is banal. We should note how these terms are invariably united about a single recurrent theme: an existence *between* realities.

As Whitman had it, echoing Matthew Arnold, "society waits unformed, and is for awhile between things ended and things begun," which is after all the quintessential American sense of history and our dubious gift to the devolution of western thought. Is it really surprising after a century of this metaphor of transition, whether in its optimistic or pessimistic forms, that after surviving innumerable redundant mock apocalypses, we should seize upon such an extreme rhetoric of desuetude?

It was not only the bomb shelter mentality of the fifties which provided us with the fashionable Apocalypse, but the Black Humor whose central tactic was, after all, to ridicule the pretensions of Existentialism by mocking the lavish redundancy of its own despair. In the sixties we hedged our bets with Entropy. Stasis seems to be in favor now. Only the degree of degradation here is different — they are all commencement exercises. "Universal History," Borges says somewhere, "is the history of the different intonations given a handful of metaphors." And now that we have scandalized ourselves in every possible way, inhabiting an incredulous world where the slightest slip of consumership can kill you, is it not appropriate to finish off these metaphors by literally beating them to death? The Apocalypse is over. Not because it didn't happen, but because it happens every day.

The eclectic, once the selection of the best from various systems, becomes atomized, free-radicalized — not even antagonistic as in dialectical thought, but a vast plurality, in which it seems each book must invent a context for itself before it can proceed. We may not be the first eclectic age; but we may be the first who knew it.

It is one thing to consider all the old rules anachronistic; it is quite another to have to invent rules as one goes along. The issue becomes very complicated here. There are those who push epistemology past Bishop Berkeley: "a kind of writing, a kind of discourse whose shape will be an interrogation, an endless interrogation of what it is doing while doing it, an endless denunciation of its fraudulence, of what it really is: an illusion (fiction) just as life is an illusion (of fiction)." (Raymond Federman)

If we make a concession to the affected view that life is only a series of endless fictions, we can also assert that the artist may — precisely because he is what he is, precisely because his willfulness *is* arbitrary — *choose* to reverse such a fashionable notion, and simply ignore the fact that "life" is patternless, while imposing coherence and order upon his narratives. No doubt he will be accused of manipulation (another word like "style" which has achieved pejorative status recently), but if Modernism proved to be over-optimistic in its attempts to reformulate the world through aesthetics, perhaps we take our own debased condition a bit too gravely. For example, from his notebooks it seems perfectly clear that Dostoevsky would agree with our contemporary view of the illusory and indeterminate quality of life, but that did not prevent him from trying to impose, as well as he could (and he always felt failure in this regard), both an inner and outer coherence in his fiction. Dostoevsky knew he was slighted, knew that the value of art in his society was changing, probably for the worse, and knew that the great mass of people with which he had such an exquisite love/hate relationship didn't give a damn about him. But he didn't expect to be invited to Stockholm to have his moral earnestness certified. Of course one might argue that he didn't have to face the *real* Modernist dilemma, that "life has changed"; but it would be difficult to substantiate that life seemed less chaotic to Dostoevsky than to us. Compared to the intellectual's despair and exhaustion on the eve of the First World War, for example, our fatigue seems fairly banal, our Agonism a bit shopworn. And to believe that our fiction is bizarre and difficult because our life is more bizarre and difficult than that of, say, Louis Phillipe's Paris, Mayhew's London, or Biely's St. Petersburg, is simply lunatic.

We are at the point where we can only dimly distinguish some broader historical outline. We know that realism requires an intimate association with historical thinking, and that it is also dependent in some direct way upon a preoccupation with the city as the engine of social life and cultural coherence. R. P. Blackmur thought, "where in 1800 the capitals of economic, political and cultural power were the same, somewhere between 1900 and 1920 they had become different. London, New York, Paris made a division of human roles. . . that has seemed in its present consequence very nearly fatal to human intelligence."

The Modernists felt themselves to be "true ancients" in the classical sense. What is unique about Post-Modernism is not its ambivalent quarrel with predecessors, which all movements share, but its refusal to resurrect and emulate a former "golden" age. Apart from the "Second Revolution," History has collapsed. It is easy to dismiss Post-Modernism's almost risible ahistoricism — seeing history primarily in terms of the evolution of aesthetic form. But we should note that the counter argument of those who seek a return to realism is severely weakened by a similar lack of historical grounding, both in their moral and philosophical precepts, as well as by virtue of the nostalgic delusion that our progenitors spent most of their leisure among books, that literature, in Emerson's words, permeated "the kitchen, the parlour, and the nursery." What is "real" about Post-Modernism is its reflection of a society which is no longer centered in any sense, much less capital centered. This recognition of a culture which can no longer be depicted by dissecting a metropolis is complemented by a view of history which resists taking a period or age as a model.

Nevertheless, to live in a time when a phenomenon such as the French "New Novel" is introduced, translated, ballyhooed, assimilated and discarded in something less than a decade, and an entire literature, previously thought to be a Spanish Colonial backwater, in the same period comes to dominate international literary consciousness, is to note that eclecticism is not without its rewards.

To see the contemporary as simply a rejection of the aesthetic moralism of Modernism is only to confuse the question. There is simply no art which does not claim, even at its most perverse, a moral dimension insofar as it is an act of free will. Even when the narrator shows his face and strings above the puppet theatre, that is a moral act, just as in the case of the narrator who announces he's going to show you how to live the second half of your life. Those who most recently rail against the Nihilism of the Post-Modern imply that we must return to conventional literary techniques to get at the truth. When Joseph Wood Krutch first complained that tragedy as we knew it is impossible in the modern world, he was above all complaining that the *shape* of Tragedy is gone. A little neo-Aristotelianism is not going to get us out of the mess we are in; the simple refusal to innovate does not produce realism, the antidote to ahistoricism is not the historical romance. In a mass society, almost any individualized resistance to the crowd, any studied articulateness, automatically confers a mild aura of counterforce, if not distinction. Even in totalitarian societies, where resistance is actually risky, to be anti-establishment, as Joseph Brodsky has pointed out, is *in itself* a moral and poetic credential, and as such encourages complacency. Cynicism, we ought to recall, exerts the most profound thought control.

The terms revolutionary and evolutionary, in their historical and scientific sense, no longer have any meaning for literary culture. The concepts of a definitive break and that of an orderly development are *both* equally foreign to us. We are dealing with rites, forms, dynamics and classifications of change for which we have no extant humanistic models. On the face of it, this would seem like a made-to-order prescription for Ford's traditional "intensive novelist," who pursues a deep inquiry into the behavior of a certain group of characters and milieu, in which the individual situation calls forth the general circumstance. Yet, the contemporary impulse, for whatever reasons, is surely to resist this kind of correspondence. The general circumstance has never been more suspect, and the impulse is to produce a literature which does not require experience to corroborate it.

What is required is a revisionist theory of Modernism which might have the following saliencies. First, regard Modernism not as a revolution, but a devolution — an open abandonment of four centuries of European aesthetic conventions — *a pathological parthenogenesis*, the purgation of any historical or symbolic contamination. This takes place in the context of the most remarkable economic growth in European history: during the fifty years before the Great War, industrial output per head grew more rapidly than before or since. It provided the technological foundation for our own century, and immeasurably increased the scope of the artist. For all its relative social inequality, this Pre-Modernist period represents the apogeé of city life, before the Bourgeois values of privacy and leisure gave way to the tempos of war. In hindsight, we have this extraordinary phenomenon of a culture being attacked as "rotten to the core," while it is now recalled as the last period of relative security and sustained accomplishment within western memory. It is unlikely that the most fervent Modernist would have wished pre-1914 Europe to disappear forever, if he had had the dimmest perception that none of the revolutions he wished for would emerge from the rubble. The most startling legacy of Modernism, in this sense, is the ferocity with which it was attacked by both Communist and National Socialist regimes. No contemporary can await the next revolution without the most profound ambivalence. It is the preeminent lesson of Modernism that antagonism is not without its costs, that cultural arrogance always seems to cut two ways.

We ought not minimize the extent to which Modernism retains the expansionist impulse of its historical era, the extent to which it is rooted in 19th century evolutionary progressivism and the concept of breakthrough. To presuppose an art which is increasingly higher, deeper, richer and more complex, is to describe a process programmed for self-destruction. This inflation of aesthetic expectations seems linked inextricably in our time to the personality which can never reach a goal — the oppressive demands of narcissism — which is what Lawrence meant when he said "we have to drop our manner of the on and on and on." The German word for this is *Totsiegen*: "winning oneself to death."

Modernism does not humanize; it pluralizes, surrealizes — this we know. Sometimes it seems the only thing we know. Yet Modernism remains essentially dialectical. For all its celebration of multiplicity it holds that anarchy can be distilled by the single aesthetic consciousness — and in this sense, contradictions remain aesthetically resolvable. It remains relatively self-policing — until, of course, the real police move in.

The exaggerations of Modernist expansionism seem almost quaint to us now. Pound's green slacks and earring are now favored by those who sell tax shelters; Stevens' blue guitar that does not play things as they are no longer seems bizarre in the hands of suburban high school girls; the most outrageous thing that could be said about crazy Marinetti was that he was the *caffeine* of Europe.

Post-Modernism is also the product of another unprecedented economic growth, American style. It is not insignificant that a graph of the consumer price index from 1930 to the present resembles exactly that of the movement of conflict, resolution and denouément of Aristotelean tragedy. As opposed to the 19th century European economic expansion, which was characterized by seventy-five years of relatively stable prices, the fluctuations in the value of money since 1914, as Keynes said, "have been on a scale so great as to constitute one of the most significant events of the modern world." These fluctuations were paralleled by an enormous expansion of the intellectual class. As Gramsci wrote, "The Democratic-Bureaucratic system has given rise to a great mass of functions which are not at all justified by the social necessities of production . . . quantity cannot be separated from quality . . . to give a democratic structure to high culture and top-level technology creates vast crises of unemployment for the middle, intellectual strata. . . . "

It is all well and good to propose art as multidimensional, requiring multichannels of communication, with process replacing analysis — but not at the expense of understanding that a multicentric culture is not only the product of aesthetic choice but of a strenuous competition between intellectuals, in which elasticity of mind, and contradictions which are more than tolerated, can be just as self-serving as the most rigid hierarchical expansionism. When the dialectic between art and history is rejected, what is also often lost is a dialectic between contemporaneous movements — which is to say, any principle of ongoing self-criticism. If every option is a mode and every mode an option, the sense of watching oneself choose can often substitute for judgment. As Gerald Graff observes, when an institution advertises as a "center" these days, you can be certain it is on the periphery. Such institutions can thrive only in a period of non-judgmentalism, which avoids *any* order or relations.

The multicentricity of culture is a contemporary fact, but the assertion that there are many centers does not ensure that there is substance in any of them. Post-Modernism harbors the deep suspicion that we have only unpleasant choices; that we may have seen the best civilization has to offer.

It should now be possible to move, if only crabwise, to a consideration of what may be culturally and aesthetically distinctive about Post-Modernist writing. The purpose of this is hardly to recommend a program, for it is precisely the programmatic nature of the "rhetoric of uniqueness" which is insufficient. It is very tiresome always to be talking about uniqueness when the issue is really one of survival. De Tocqueville saw that democratic society was at once "exciting and monotonous," for behind "every insistence upon uniqueness" there lay the "terror of stasis and of missed opportunity." Or, as Jacques Riviére pointed out to Antonin Artaud — there is a "vast contrast between the extraordinary precision of your self-diagnosis, and the vagueness of what you are endeavoring to achieve."

II.

7. Opacity as Reality

Philosophy is a noble and arduous discipline. Fiction is equally severe. But literary philosophy is shit. Literary Sociology is shit. Literary Psychology is shit. What would a literary physics be? . . . I tried to write a book that would not be like all the books I despise.

—*William Gass,* a letter

William Gass is the only contemporary American writer who has given us a coherent philosophy of fiction, an aesthetics which he actually practices, and a criticism coextensive with his art. His approach is apparently Formalist — tough-minded, polemical, proceeding through the entire panoply of relativism to purge the sentimental impulse — so that in the end the performance can be reaffirmed in impassioned holistic assertion:

> A consciousness electrified by beauty — is that not the aim and emblem of the ending of all finely made love?

> Are you Afraid? *[Fiction and the Figures of Life]*

It requires considerable contrariness to use such words unself-consciously, and a summary of Gass's concerns illustrates an operational, if still largely unspoken, consensus among a great many contemporary writers.

Fiction does not render the world but makes its own world. Fiction is not history because history itself cannot be understood in itself as a language, as history does not consist of signs. Further, history is not intelligible without an extra-historical essence as a matter of principle. Therefore, fiction presumes an epistemologically *privileged* position as a matter of course. It operates as a distinct and whole addition to reality; in this sense, fiction *always* challenges conventional reality. Yet fiction is a world which *can* be entered, and against which one can measure oneself. In such a world, plot and characterization are only vestiges ("mostly canvas") of historical recall, less important to narrative momentum than we suppose. For the basic literal component here is the sentence, and it is the *drama of sentences*, formed more by the ear than eye, closer to poetry than to exposition, which forms the true momentum of narrative, a series of choices made from the possibilities of language, "a world inseparable from its language," in which style *is* significance.

The reader is not a passive participant in this enterprise, any more than the narrator is a passive observer of reality. To reverse the commonly received notion, the work is the judge of the reader. "The purpose of a literary work is the capture of consciousness, and the consequent creation in you, of an imagined sensibility." *In you* is operative here. Demands are placed upon the reader which simply don't exist in the traditional literary transaction, implying that the reader must justify *his* own existence.

There is nothing here that would be foreign to the oldest of the New Critics. But the Formalist program is modified in several significant aspects.

First of all, what the New Critical Formalists did for poetry, Gass does for fiction. Whereas the traditional Formalists were more concerned with laying out an idealistic charter to preserve conservative values, liberate the idea of coherence from historical scholars, and oppose the nihilistic experimentation and futurism of the Avant-Garde, Gass's idealism takes a much more aggressive form, where the reader is not merely asked to lay aside certain preconceptions, but to put himself on the line, to overcome the fear of the strange "other life" which language offers. The implication is, simply, why would anyone want fiction to be synchronous with the real world?

With Gass, early Modernism has been fully assimilated, and as such formalism is no longer predicated upon a doctrinal sense of loss, but rather upon a new set of contractual relations. This takes traditional formalism beyond its own compulsive dualism to insist upon a true reciprocity not between word and thing, but between reader and writer. Fiction *is* a simulacrum of reality at some point, but it is not achieved through a system of value, or a formula for feelings; it is a process of signification which does not unify experiences but is its own experience. The work of art can only be experienced as original — never representative. This is quite the opposite of Barth. Rather than "exposing" artifice, the writer must overcome the reader's suspicion of the "artificial," recapture him in an absolute reorganization.

Philosophically, this may be very old hat; it is original only in the lyricism of its presentation and its spirit of affirmation.* Rather than lamenting the departure of good readers (and reality itself), Gass insists that if the writer is true to his privileged position, then the reader *can* be recaptured. Rather than merely insult the reader, Gass urges him on a very exacting journey — which in our time may amount to the same thing. To make such demands on the reader is, in one sense, to make a virtue of necessity, which is the essential formalist anomaly. The reader, like the book itself, is idealized — beyond history.

The unspoken enemy of fiction throughout Gass's work is not Realism *per se* but what André Gide's Edouard called the "tyranny of resemblance":

> It is because the novel of all literary *genres* is the freest, the most *lawless*, . . . it is for that very reason, for fear of that very liberty (the artists who are always sighing after liberty are often the most bewildered when they get it), that the novel has always clung to reality with such timidity. And I am not speaking only of the French novel. It is the same with the English novel; and the Russian novel, for all its throwing off of constraints, is a slave to resemblance. The only progress it looks to is to get still nearer to nature. A novel has never known that 'formidable erosion of contours' as Nietzsche calls it; that deliberate avoidance of life, which gave style to the works of the Greek dramatists, for instance, or to the tragedies of the French 17th Century. Is there anything more perfectly and deeply human than these works? But that's just it — they are human only in their depth; they don't pride themselves on appearing so — or, at any rate, on appearing real. *[The Counterfeiters]*

---

*One of the problems with Gass's argument is that it is so easily vulgarized; e.g.: "Superfiction does not represent reality. It does not recreate reality . . . Instead it creates a whole life of its own . . . with all the energy, playfulness, and exuberance that we associate with the best times of living, here under the control of a master creator, the fictionist. It's the difference between watching the neighbors and having your own fun. . . . " [J. Klinkowitz, *The Life of Fiction*]

Mark Schorer amplifed this contemporary prejudice, as early as 1948:

> When we speak of technique, we speak of nearly everything. The difference between content, or experience, and achieved content for art, is technique. For technique is the means by which the writer's experience, which is his subject matter, compels him to attend to it: technique is the only means he has of discovering, exploring, developing his subject, of conveying its meaning, and finally of evaluating it.
>
> Technique alone objectifies the materials of art: hence technique alone evaluates those materials. This is the axiom which demonstrates itself so devastatingly whenever a writer declares under the urgent sense of the importance of his materials — whether these are autobiography, or social ideas or personal passions — whenever such a writer declares that he cannot linger with technical refinements. ["Technique as Discovery"]

While the theoreticians' view of art is nominally one of constraints and conventions, the writer *always* has a choice, a choice that he does not have as a mere man, for only as a writer can he become the totally self-referential narrator of *Willie Masters' Lonesome Wife*, or the abstract third balcony baritone of *Omensetter's Luck*, who chooses to speak to us in a *patois* of midwestern rural vernacular, often cast in iambic pentameter. It is this matter of genuine, if arbitrary choice, so crucial to the artist, that critics so often miss, what Gass describes as the "*kindly* imprisonment" of the literary. The constraints of this prison are far different than those of the Structuralist penitentiary, where Language is seen as a vicious circle, literally signifying nothing except itself, the exaggeration *pro forma* of man's condition — all speech hyperbole, all prose rhetorical, all poetry prosedemic, all thought proleptic.

While it is true that we are circumscribed by language, it is simply a matter of rhetoric — not as a series of devices, but a spectrum of choices — whether we choose to describe that circle as vicious or magical. It is here that we must either confess with Pascal and Rousseau that we are trapped within language and dignify silence as the only nobility, or reassert a faith in the plasticity of life, in its linguistic possibilities, as did Nietzsche and William James. There are those who *choose* to be lost, locked into an "ontology of nothingness," though we ought not forget that reports from "the void" are just as unverifiable as those from safer regions, and probably less so. Just because we hate ourselves does not mean we still are not living a lie. The realization of "nothingness" is one thing — like going into a room and reporting that "nothing is there" — but one cannot begin at the beginning of nothingness any more than one can start at the beginning of any learning process. One cannot make assertions about language or nature from a hypothetical vantage point outside them. That is why it is nonsense to postulate an "entrapment within language," since there is no vantage from which anyone could possibly know that. The only thing that is sensorily certain about language is that when we're in it, we're also out of it; and when we're out of it, we are still aware of ourselves in it.

For Gass, the crisis of culture is a crisis of language, and the solution is neither silence nor the decontrol of an elusive social reality, but the exploitation of the natural force of language in its own right. It is precisely because language outlives itself that it is eventually subject to mastery. Gass can make this assertion only by side-stepping one of the oldest and most difficult of linguistic problems — that of reference. No one knows how language hooks in to the real world. But Gass gets off the hook by pronouncing this a non-problem — the fact that we don't know, doesn't mean that we are done for. It is a 20th century solution par excellence; a philosophically inadequate world is more than compensated for by an adequate aesthetic world. Gass leaves no doubt that this trade-off is salutary; yet his admirable eloquence does not finally dispel our doubts that aesthetics can get us all the way home.

There is an epistemological shift here which in its stupefying simplicity ought not to be overlooked. As each age defines its own reality, each reveals its own preference of perspective, often influenced by technology. The 18th century, for example, was extremely fond of the telescope and its imagery, but ridiculed the microscope. The 20th century has its own ambivalent obsession with the camera, which ends up in our time dividing works into those written primarily to be adapted for film, and those whose primary status seems utterly to resist visual translation. At any rate, if we simply imagine, in Ortega's figure, a man looking out of his window at a garden, it doesn't take a genius to note the shift from the objective integrity of the 18th century framed landscape — through the implosion of the frame in the 19th century in which the reality of the garden is sharply attenuated as the focus of the observer comes to the fore — to the present, in which the "window" is neither transparent nor mirrored, but a membrane simultaneously separating and connecting perceiver and object, fogged with authorial breath as much as nature's mist. This 20th century metaphor for language is a cognitive process in which *both* man and garden are not only in reduced perspective, but cannot be said to exist independently of the process. The window of language is no longer in fact a window, but its own autotelic agency: Opacity as Reality.*

No one knows why each historical period chooses to change the emphasis of the equation, but the writer ought to be aware of his choice of epistemology, for it is just as determining, or perhaps even more so, than the prepackaged social categories (manners) and predetermined significance (genre) which he finds so despicably shopworn. Moreover, if classical periods can be said to thrive upon the moral sense, and the 19th century upon the metaphysical, then Post-Modernism has ideologized the epistemological. It mimicks not History, but Philosophy.

Gass's achievement is the recognition that if language is the distinctive feature of human behavior, and if our choice of epistemology is wholly arbitrary, then one can take a celebratory rather than a deterministic view of language, by asserting that experience is simply not sufficient for creating knowledge of the real world, unless structures are vested to incorporate that experience through conscious aesthetic arrangement. "It is the sentence which confers reality upon certain relations, but it also controls one's estimation, apprehension and response to them." This is a compelling notion because it relies neither on solipsistic determinism nor the concept of aesthetic "breakthrough." It insists that the work of art is a system fully complete at any one moment, a perpetual present, no matter how much extrinsic factors may affect its past and future. A story is not "fictionalized," or "life-like"; it is a fiction with a life of its own. This is a crucial distinction because it does not deny reality to objects which have an ontological status outside of language. Indeed, Gass is typically indifferent to this question. He is simply lyrically and aggressively reaffirming Fry's

---

*This philosophical debate is not amplified by advances in neurophysiology. The animal retina is clearly not a passive transmitter of information, but a highly discriminatory faculty, which means the most elementary act of perception is inextricably tied up with learning and memory — evidence certainly for the Formalist contention that reality is conditioned by technique. Yet the Realist can point out that the reorganization by the optic nerve involves a mere three synapses, that any degeneration of precision is quite minor, and the statistical reliability of the process is intact and purposive. We are not much advanced in this regard since Poe noted that "we always see too little, but we always see too much."

distinction between the rocking horse and the derby winner's photo, while dismissing the kind of fiction which *always* predominates in the culture — a literature which rehearses currently popular ideas and serves them up as reality, with little regard for artistic quality and originality.

Be that as it may, one can legitimately ask why we need such an elaborate and fully pressed theory to combat so perennial and so obvious a problem? The nagging suspicion of the Post-Modern is that by being so conspicuously on guard against a potentially compromised aesthetic, so conscious of avoiding the Realist commonplace, we retreat again into another version of "can't go backness" — applied in this case to temporal reality as Barth applies it to history itself. This is a program which sanctifies risk, yet in its denial of the relevance of external judgment, has in fact nothing to lose. As with Avant Garde, the adversaries it locates in the conventional world are never concretized, and its rhetoric of autonomy becomes as standardized as that of those over-administered hierarchies it presumably negates.

For if the artist is as free as Gass insists, why must he expend so much energy in subliminally fending off inferior art? "To see the garden," he says, "and to see the glass in the window pane are two incompatible operations." Yet if the artist does assume an epistemologically privileged position, this problem should be surmountable in the sense that the artist can erase, renegotiate, or ignore boundaries with the same assurance he draws them.

It is characteristic of the Formalist impulse, and typical of so much contemporary art, that we can admire it without being finally convinced of its necessity. For here we have a system without leaks or levers; literature as a closed organism, a factory in which curiosity about what is fabricated and what is the goal of its labor are apparently questions outside its design.

Gass raises the question whether an aesthetic so fully and systematically engaged against Pseudo-art allows itself the amplitude to authenticate itself. It exudes that uneasiness peculiar to all movements which attempt to fulfill heroic cultural models independent of society, an art which presents itself through pure expressivity as an idealized form in which content is secondary.

8. To Drain a Lake

If you drain a lake, the water must run somewhere. If it is no longer where it used to be, where has it gone? Where can it go?

—*Saul Bellow*

If William Gass insists upon the primacy of language in its most idealistic form, then Saul Bellow is certainly our most consistent advocate of the realistic tradition; indeed, his view of society as a noetic domain fully available to conventional literary embodiment approaches something of an obsession. Nowhere in contemporary literature is the uneasy and anomic relationship between the writer and his critical audience, between the artist and his antecedents, more apparent than in the career of Saul Bellow. No other writer has so fully exploited the type of the modern intellectual, with such attendant scorn for the implications of the type.

Bellow's uniqueness and strength has always been that he, practically alone, focuses on the *continuity* of the 19th century novel, rather than on the Grand Caesura of Modernism. While his work is often concerned with the most up-to-date ideas and preoccupations, never is there a single concession to Modernist aesthetic experimentation — nowhere else is Modernism discoursed upon in such an amodernist mode. In fact, most of Bellow's work may be seen as a threnody on the disappearance of homogeneous cultural quality and unity, the attenuation of the actual. Bellow's realism is not so much an aesthetic program as a habit of mind, an implicit value system of bourgeois individualism which will not accede to the individual's diminishment. "It is the Self, the person to whom things happen, who is perhaps not acceptable to the difficult and fastidious Modern consciousness."

And clearly, insofar as Bellow's protagonists are victims, it is not as a result of an uxorious fate or existential dilemma, but because they spend so much time rehashing, revising, and discarding the innumerable fashionable vocabularies of self-description which our century demands of them. Here the self, as well as the narrator, is gained by *shedding* intellectual baggage, the irony being that what is shed nevertheless seems to be the substance of the work; culture is what one remembers after one forgets all the books one has read.

There are two historical facts here which both those who overpraise Bellow for his "serious intellectualizing," and those who damn him for his old-fashioned, plotted prose, altogether miss.

First is Bellow's acute awareness that the 19th century novel was central to the creation of mass culture, a fact which no amount of modernist elitism can entirely minimize. Secondly, Bellow's own career, like Gass's, roughly spans the time between the last phase of high, Modernist culture, those writers who made a claim upon consciousness by insisting that *only* art endured, and the present situation where the printed word has been inexorably removed to the periphery of the culture, where the writer is no longer sage, and does not even inspire any particular celebrity. In this vacuum, our present diminished author must deal with the dark side of Modernism, the nagging possibility that he has somehow lost not only his audience, but also centuries of inherited forms of communication. It is indicative that Bellow constantly attempts to smuggle 19th century authority into the cerebralized novel, while always skeptical of skepticism as the modern orthodoxy, which is no mean feat. His work is testimony to how far one can go in our time by simply refusing to be cute.

This view of the lost 19th century audience, of an entire civilization poring over narratives by lamplight, of a novel in every picnic hamper, must be contrasted with Gass's supreme indifference to such an audience. But who is to blame for this loss of audience, if not the author? If Gass locates the crisis in language, Bellow blames the culture, generally — *very* generally:

> Art must be understood as a purgation of consciousness. Among the things to be purged are the latest infections, the poisons of the sophisticated media. Can this be done? Well, I don't know. By ordinary means? I don't know that either. But one must have some very powerful command of one's art in order to cope with this invasion of foreign bodies. [Interview]

What I am trying to indicate is that cultural style is not to be confused with genuine understanding. At the moment, such understanding has few representatives, while cultural style seems to have hundreds of thousands. ["Literature in the Age of Technology"]

This then is the situation. Critics and professors have declared themselves the true heirs and successors of the modern classic writers. They have obscured the connection between the contemporary writer and his predecessors. They have not shaped the opinions of the educated classes. They have miseducated the young. ["Cloister Culture"]

Elsewhere he complains that Dickens didn't try to be John Stuart Mill, though Bellow is painfully aware of how much closer Dickens and Mill were than, say, Bellow and Harold Bloom. It is no accident that *Mr. Sammler's Planet* is by far Bellow's most fully realized work, because we have a narrator who is finally comfortable with himself, a figure who has always lurked in the heart of Bellow's characterizations, the Professor Manqué.

We can have no more dissimilar reactions to contemporary experience and its potential literary embodiment than those of Bellow and Donald Barthelme. Compare Barthelme's parody of Henry James:

Try to be a man about whom nothing is known, our father said, when we were young. Our father said several other interesting things, but we have forgotten what they were . . . Our father was a man about whom nothing was known. Nothing is known about him still. He gave us the recipes. He was not very interesting. A tree is more interesting. A sentence is more interesting. A canned good is more interesting . . . *[Snow White]*

with the solemnity of Sammler:

He was aware that he must meet, and he did meet —through all the confusion and degraded clowning of this life through which we are speeding — he did meet the terms of his contract. The terms of which in his inmost heart, each man knows, as I know mine. As all know. For that is the truth of it — that we all know, God, that we know, that we know, we know, we know.

The total divergence, in every possible respect, of two writers in the same time and place, is worthy of our awe, and perhaps only awe.

Sammler's complaint represents the culmination of twenty years of Bellow's expository occasional pieces, which are really a series of Sammler-like rhetorical questions on the theme, "What is to be done?" It is rather as if Bellow as critic were the straight man for Bellow the novelist.

Perhaps some power within us will tell us what we are, now that the old misconceptions have been laid low. Undeniably the human being is not what he commonly thought a century ago. The question nevertheless remains. He is *something*.* What is he? ["Recent American Fiction"]

Now realism in literature is convention and this convention postulates that human beings are not what everyone for long centuries conceived them to be. They are *something* different, and they live in a disenchanted world that exists for no particular purpose that science can show. ["Machines & Storybooks"]

At the moment, however, the writer feels a certain inferiority. He inherits a realistic tradition in which the writer deals in facts and seems to know. But *what sort* of knowledge does he actually have? . . . Writers cannot simply continue in the old way. ["The Writer as Moralist"]

I cannot agree with recent writers who have told us that we are nothing. We are indeed not what The Golden Ages boasted us to be. But we are *something*. ["Fiction of the Fifties"]

Something was being done to put in question the meaning of survival, the meaning of pity, the meaning of justice and of the importance of being oneself. ["Literature in the Age of Technology"]

The novel can't be compared to the epic, or to the monuments of poetic drama. But it is the best we can do just now. It is sort

*Emphasis added.

of a latterday lean-to, a hovel in which the spirit takes
shelter . . . it tells us that for every human being there is a diversity
of existences, that the single existence is itself an illusion in part,
and that these many existences signify *something*, fulfill
something . . . [Nobel Speech]

One's reaction to this is comparable to Tolstoy's response to a poem
of Maeterlinck's he couldn't fathom. "Who went out? Who came in?
Who is speaking? Who died?"

The acknowledgement that something *has* happened is circumscribed
by the more frightening notion that something *hasn't* happened — that
there have been substantive changes in human character which are not
expressed in theories of aesthetic innovation, that there *are* continuities
in the human condition and the realist's perception of it which have
not been spelled out, much less reaffirmed. In both its vagueness and
assertiveness, this constitutes an all too familiar contemporary view of
History — culminating in the writer who through some unparticularized
conspiracy of intellectuals has been denied not only his audience but
his very tradition; that Lake which has dried up, but is still *somewhere*!
How does one attack intellectual inauthenticity if one's own means and
materials are indistinguishable from those of the intellectuals one is
attacking? How does one account for the recent changes in the human
condition, and also imply that the radical aesthetic procedures which
paralleled them are irrelevant? If we can't continue "in the same old
way," then why does Bellow do it?

The suspicion persists that what Bellow is attempting to recapture
is not Realism, nor a newly efficacious method, but rather the centrality
of the realist writer in an integrated and properly honorific culture.
What is being expressed is the fear that no matter how relentlessly
serious one is, that no matter how forcefully one resists the gimmickry
of Modernism, History itself — that sedimentary outline of the great
lake — has denied him the possibility of being taken seriously. It is
this fear, the fear of the *Epigonentum* — of living in a totally derivative
age — which makes Bellow's work, at first glance so aesthetically timid,
so quintessentially Post-Modern: the last thing he ever wanted.

Against Bellow's obsessions with lost audience, shattered authority,
corrupt intermediaries, and that redundant, ineffable "*something*," the
loss of which is all the more poignant in its lack of specificity, we may
place Gass's idea of art as its own independent reality, a form which
is neither ahistorical nor rehearsed history, a willed achievement

apparently as indifferent to its sources as to its effect. It should not be surprising that both writers locate Pseudo-Art in the *other's* tradition, or that the strategy in both cases is one of recapture. Gass's response is to take the aesthetics of Formalism to a fully blown affirmative conclusion: Technique as Absolute, literature as a cultural object which transcends and transforms History.

In his suspicion of Formalist orthodoxy, Bellow might have debated this question, for his own bourgeois realism surely implies that the repository of history can determine style. Yet he himself is unable to locate the "lost content" which his method presumably champions, that lost content which in fact *is* his basic subject matter.

Gass's argument is more felicitous, but not necessarily superior; it simply lacks Bellow's resentment and bitterness. If Gass sees the problem as one of the lay reader confusing fiction with History, and would make every reader an intellectual, Bellow sees his own middlebrow audience as compromised by a conspiracy of intellectuals. (It is a commonplace of Post-Modernism that the barbarism once attributed to the provincial middle-class is shifted to intellectuals as their status becomes increasingly respectable.) Bellow sees himself (correctly in this case) as denied both the mantle of the Modernist giants *as well* as the imprimatur of the Vanguard, which, infuriatingly enough, puts him in the company of practically everyone else.

When all is said and done, this is not a proper philosophical debate at all. At the most basic level of analysis, Bellow simply prefers a narrative style closer to human speech, while Gass relies on more sonorous and poetic devices, style as both a mask and admission. What it boils down to is Gass's absorption of the late Modernist aesthetic — the peripherality of the artist is precisely what gives him his leverage — set alongside of Bellow's sense that "something" has pushed the writer out of his centrality, and that the resultant distancing amounts only to a dissipation of power. They are both right, as far as it goes.

But if Gass is occasionally ethereal, Bellow is from the first evasive, ranting against those intellectuals who have done art a disservice. "The fact is that modern art has tried very hard to please its intellectual judges. . . . Art in the 20th century is more greatly appreciated if it is directly translatable into intellectual interests, if it lends itself to discourse. Because intellectuals do not like to suspend themselves in works of the imagination. They prefer to talk." ["Machines and Storybooks"] There could not be a more withering indictment of his own work.

Bellow's poignancy is characteristic of the Realist Revivalist in an officially Modernist culture. Realizing quite appropriately that the predominance of technique cannot be assuaged by yet another technique, that it is necessary to posit a Humanism to which technique is subordinated, he can nevertheless offer only pious verbalisms scarcely above the level of the man in the street. The Formalist bias, despite its clear limitations, can no longer be countered by a simple appeal to admissable content.

9. Rouse the Stupid and Damp the Pert

I had been plotting arch romance without knowing it.

—*Henry James*

The absolute killer is not to have a sense of humor.

—*Johnny Carson*

What most obviously distinguishes recent American fiction not only from its predecessors but also from its world counterparts is the relentless seriousness and protoplasmic energy of its humor. As Sinclair Lewis says of his dear Babbitt, "he had felt that he had been cast into that very net from which he had with such fury escaped, and supremest jest of all, had been made to rejoice in the trapping," a comment which might be applied equally to contemporary narrators. We know that we lack the light vein — the gentle wit of the English, the acerbity of the French, the allegorical irony of the central European. We know how much of a dead end is our tradition of the tall tale, which is simply the vernacular gone hyperbolic. How then to account for the potentiating levity of our current literature? Certainly our times are not as vaudevillian as our novels make out; we have an extraordinarily difficult time with our politics, puerile as they may be. And certainly one of Classic Modernism's central features is its quintessential humorlessness, particularly as regards its own procedures. It will be very difficult for the next generation to understand the measure of hatred directed at the Bourgeoisie of Europe in the first decades of this century. The reaction will seem as overblown and remote as the repentant manners of the Russian aristocracy. The very reading aloud of the stentorian Eliot or Pound these days is often enough to elicit a guffaw. This is not the trivialized mockery which pervades popular culture, weatherwoman ribbing anchorman, or the studied self-deprecation which seems to be our newest sales technique. It is a highly conditional and often cheerless jocularity, what the Germans call *Witzelsucht*, a pathological compulsion to make jokes in inappropriate situations at the expense of others.

Coextensive with Modernism's high seriousness, we were heir also to the apotheosis of Existentialism. Huizinga warned as early as 1936: "the next addition to the collection of fashionable words will be 'existential'." "Black humor" functioned chiefly as a parody and counterweight to apocalyptic existentialism, as if someone had put sunglasses and jogging shoes on Camus' *Sisyphus*. As Ronald Tavel put it in the Sixties, to label his wacky theatrics, "our position is no longer absurd; it is simply ridiculous."

In this sense Post-Modernism exploits the gap (crevasse is perhaps a better word) between the abstraction of literary discourse and what's left of the felt life. The incongruities here are so often bloated that they make the old word-is-not-the-thing argument almost trivial in its obviousness, and a perfect subject for comic exploitation. The oxymoronic of the everyday, which used to be confined chiefly to politicians and corporate Public Relations men, has evolved a jargon (better yet, a *meta*-language) for every profession and lifestyle — adolescent, businessman, street person, intellectual, housewife, militant, druggie, new woman, country boy, *et al.*, dialects which are immediately encrypted by the media, and thus circulate through the culture by reverse loop so that the stereotype, linguistically speaking, is "real people" — dialects so circumscribed as to make those of the old European class system seem rich, strange and exotic. When such a "real person" is encountered in real life, the first reaction is parody, and to the objection that we miss the old-fashioned rounded fictional character standing four square between the narrator and the reader, one can only reply that from the contemporary perspective the contemporary character's one-dimensionality is precisely what is *most* real about him. We have here a people whose social identity and psychology is not something to be inferred from their speech but *is* their speech.

Of this new humor there are many variations:

Humor that fails deliberately: 1,300 one-liners is an excuse for a narrative. The strategy here is redundancy; making a bad joke, then deprecating the audience for not realizing it was an intentional bad joke, hence, finally getting an embarrassed laugh.

The put on: In Jacob Brackman's phrase: "neither parody nor satire which are rigorous demanding forms . . . by not holding any real position, one is invulnerable to attack. . . . aggressive ambiguity, the strategy of which is not to be ironic but confusing in a faintly amusing way." It limits the good nature of the perpetrator as well as the distrust and skepticism of the beholder.

Humor as evasion: Terror of reality. Mockery as avoidance of concrete confrontation or analysis. Wisecrack as the refuge of the powerless.

Humor as wit: Replacing strength as the primary means of impressing another. Everybody his own comedian. "I may not be authentic, but I'm a good listener."

Pathos: To be truly sad and silly at the same time; not as easy as it sounds. "Seriously though. . . let's stop kidding around. . ."

Humor as sublimated aggression: attacking the epistemological ground of the reader, venality attacking vacuity, intimidating the reader with his own sense of instability.

Humor as defiance: anti-pietistic, and even occasionally heroic. As the Viennese jokesmith who pronounced America a mistake, a *big* mistake, notes: "one refuses to go under suffering, activates the ego against the real world, and victoriously upholds the pleasure principle, yet all without quitting the grounds of mental sanity." [Freud, *On Humor*, 1920]

It is a commonplace that humor in America has moved from that based on innocence to a savage sophistication, a culture in which everyone knows too much. Even writers as recent as Hemingway and Fitzgerald in retrospect seem utterly innocent beings in their romances, and Twain's sarcasm positively good-hearted. Richard Poirier has noted the advent of parody parodying itself as it goes along, calling into question "the activity itself of creating any literary form. . . ." *[A World Elsewhere]*

But there is more to it than this. The hallmark of a Barthelme story, for example, whatever its quality, is that it is *essentially unparodyable.* Think of the consequences of that — anticipating every objection in its very rhythms, a work of art which will not yield to further mimicry. Within its own context it can only be imitated: neither totally assimilated nor challenged; the *ne plus ultra* of daemonic irony, the end of the road of interiority.

Constance Rourke in her classic study of American humor in 1931 saw even then—when American literature was still in awe of English literature—this obsession with native humor, and its potential to be a "fashioning instrument. . . holding tenuously to the spread elements of national life." Also, "the American character is still split into many characters. . . the comic upset has often relaxed rigidities which might have been more significant if taut; individualism has sometimes seemed to wear away under a prolonged common laughter. The solvent of humor has often become a jaded formula, the comic rebound automatic—'laff that off'—so that only the uneasy habit of laughter appears with acute sensitivity and insecurity beneath it, as though too much had been laughed away. . . The Comic rejoinder has become every man's tool." She goes on to say that "the epical promise has never been completely fulfilled. Though extravagance has been a major element in all American comedy, though extravagance may have its incomparable uses with flights and inclusions denied the more equable view, the extravagant vein in American humor has reached no ultimate expression."

It is clear that with the Post-Modern, the "extravagant vein" *has* certainly reached a kind of "ultimate expression." While increasingly puerile in many forms, such humor nevertheless represents an astonishing aesthetic response to modern life. Twain himself noted that English comedy and French wit were dependent upon their *subject matter*, while American humor relied upon the *manner* of its telling. Barthelme has largely succeeded in parodying *both* the Holy Technique of Gass as well as the Humanist Verbalism of Bellow, standing High Modernism on its head.

Such a clear culmination of national humor, in its melancholy travesty, underscores a culture on the knife edge. "The comic comes into being," Henri Bergson notes, "when society and the individual, freed from the worry of self-preservation, begin to regard *themselves* as works of art." And ironic humor as the primary convention of aesthetic behavior comes into being when Realism and Formalism, equally plagued by self-doubt, exaggerate their claims and invite the burlesque of all real things.

III.

10. The Indeterminist Fallacy

I am capable of conceiving of a writer of today, who simply cannot understand, and who has never been able to understand, what his fellow writers are driving at . . .

—*Malcolm Lowry*

The contemporary assertion that language is not only constitutive of reality but is its *own* reality continues to go unquestioned, even as it leaves the philosophical question begging. For how are we to comprehend something which is totally autonomous? A truly autonomous language could convey no human relations whatsoever.

There are, at the least, two extreme versions of this assertion. The first is the all too familiar one, which textualists have taken over with a vengeance, that is, the demythification and deconstruction of art, usually accompanied by the rhetoric of insurrection: "Since literature's own viable status is a subversion, its function can only be a terrorizing one . . . of burning/consuming meaning. By this act, the reading/writing process makes manifest the possibility of meaning." (Jacques Ehrmann) One can only suggest that anyone who has ever set pen to paper knows that this is not empirically descriptive of anyone's cognitive process, no matter how burned out he may be. It is never clear in such pyrotechnics just *who* is being subverted.

Or what is one to make of this state of affairs?

Since it is true that man is a semiotic structure and since language and man are essentially reified refractions of images endlessly succeeding each other in textuality, one might say that "man" is perplexed, puzzled, by the "tyrannical feed back system" of his knowledge, which hints that he and his actions might be only

a set of reflecting and replicating signs drawn off into the infinitude of the parallax, "the eternal ongoing rush of discourse."
[William Spanos, Paul Bové and Daniel O'Hara, *The Question of Textuality*]

Perplexed and puzzled indeed! It is typical of Post-Modernism to inflate the riskiness of the literary impulse in exact proportion to literature's diminishing influence; a quite peculiar but very contemporary combination of simultaneous hubris and abjection.

The theoretical appeal of Structuralism or Textualism is undeniably powerful, as it proposes to relocate in language those structures which the realist tradition located (and somehow lost) in the objective world. The presumption is that we are dealing with an unconscious which is not only collective, but can be collected because it is structured like a language. In this sense, it is difficult to imagine a method which has promised more and whose results have been more inconclusive. Given the regularity with which structures have failed to emerge, the response is predictable — the culture is a conspiracy which refuses to reveal itself, and art is nothing more than windowless epidemia.

In this sense, Textualism throws onto language all those determinisms which Marx and Freud sought to locate in history or the psyche — language being a symbolic net which cuts us off from our origins, a series of analogies with no instrumental relation to the world. Language is what veils the truth, and our only hope is that it veils it *systematically*. Textualism betrays both an incurable nostalgia for some kind of prelinguistic paradise and an apocalyptic view of the future. We can agree that language can be reduced to formal models which have no universal or synthetic consequences. Further, we can agree that words cut us off from our origins and have no direct instrumental relation to the world. But we can also insist that professional detachment, literary or otherwise, is no cure for alienation. Exposing one's ignorance and limitations cannot be justified as either scientific or therapeutic. The split between sensation and thinking is not a "frame of reference" to be solved by "interdisciplinary studies." It is actually quite painful. The absurd is not the amusing theatre we have made it.

Just as ethical action cannot be deduced from any situation without some value beyond reason, why describe a world of signifiers as malignant rather than magical, in the terminology of circumscription rather than access? "For them the block which language piles up before the expression of undiminished experience becomes an altar," Adorno tells us. "The disproportion between language and the rationalized society drives the authentics to plunder language, rather than drive it on, through greater sharpness, to its proper due." Indeed, the more ambitious and sophisticated the critical method, the more it appropriates the world through linguistics, the more it seems to confirm the essential mystery, not to mention the relative lucidity of literature.

An ancillary argument gone full circle, often adopted by fiction writers, is the insistence that life too is a fiction, albeit not necessarily a particularly readable one — so that life, like "reality," begins to appear in quotes. This is all harmless in its way, as novelists are notoriously (and necessarily) limited epistemologists, though more often than not, the result sidesteps the problem of trying to distinguish value in texts — an act which is not only "critical," but implicitly *every* author's, the moment he begins another book. The fact remains that many "texts" actually captivate, take us over, and we are to some extent remade through them. This strangely persistent fact of a text's social presence is one which the Textualist argument seeks to ignore, for reasons which are not entirely clear. But the predominant notion of the "equality" of texts, literature as only a text in the world among others, testifies to the bankruptcy of language. As Gerald Graff puts the matter succinctly:

> The degeneration of public language into cliché as a consequence of propaganda, publicity, advertising and academese has had far ranging consequences for modern literature. The immediate consequences of this situation — in which literature finds itself virtually deprived of uncontaminated language — have been negative; literature either depends excessively upon private myth and the structures of the "mythical method," or else, turning against myth, becomes anti-literature, venting scorn on itself as a kind of punishment for its continued dependence on an exhausted and discredited language. *[Literature Against Itself]*

While it isn't necessary to rehearse instances of this, it is worth pointing out that one way to deal with the problem is to make deteriorated language the *subject* of one's writing; the incorporation of *dreck* in order to expose it. Like any one-track strategy, however, this one obviously has severe intrinsic limitations, degenerating into mere disenchantment with forms, the inability to produce anything but

purely static works of art, devolving often into what Georg Lukács
called that "cynical laughter which is its own subject, which pervades
everything and effects nothing." *[The Meaning of Contemporary
Realism]*

Nevertheless, if we are prepared to accept meaning which is not
"immanent" in history *or* language, and hence not strictly discoverable,
but the fruit of an ongoing if finally inexplicable collaboration between
the mind and the world, then we can project upon human history the
only meaning it can possibly have — which is precisely what literature
aims for in its extra-historical, extra-cultural, and extra-psychological
assertiveness.

In such a situation, the reader is challenged to be sure, but the idea
is to *captivate* the reader by whatever means necessary. The writer
through the assertion of epistemologically privileged authority invites
the reader to become a dilettante — not in the current pejorative sense,
but in the sense of the original Latin root, *delectare*, "to take delight
in." This is a far cry from the pessimistic, deterministic vision of
language as entrapment — though that vision can also be derived from
the same argumentative principles of language as the ultimate reality.
The power of speech can affirm and expand the existence of the
language animal; the necessity to write "in order," as Le Clezio says,
"to conquer the silence of other languages." Indeed, Textualist ideology actually refuses this kind of meaning, since the metaphor for
its own activity is *dispersal*, the impossibility of unity. It is a short step
from the notion of discredited languages to the idea of language itself
as exhausted, from a plurality of meanings to the absence of meaning,
but this logic ignores the quite unphilosophical fact that most writers
necessarily believe, unsystematically and unskeptically, in a language
which is forever in process; language as activity, not doctrine.

It is easy to forget just how much precision and pleasure literary
language can afford; at any rate such a notion is apparently nothing
upon which to build a career. It used to be that writers fought for access
to privileged ground. The competition now seems to be for that terrain
which is the swampiest. Textualism takes the disjunction between
ordinary and literary discourse — a phony contrast between an
unmediated vision of the real, and the way we actually speak — and
inflates it to the status of a universal metaphor. Textualism refuses the
essential pragmatism of the creative process, and subjects it to an
impossible redemption. There is no going back to a prelinguistic

paradise, to a supremacy over time based upon some primordial stupidity, any more than we can decay into a future McLuhanite garden of undifferentiated consciousness, an apotheosis of silence where we can treat our wordlessness as innocence. And the writer's only dignity is that he should know this better than anyone, that in his peculiar isolation he stands for all men.

Textualism, in effect, marks the end of the Second Revolution, in which the secondary languages developed to counter Bourgeois subjectivity become irrelevant to the analysis of actual conditions, the obsession with paradigm obscuring both art and experience. Textualism not only forfeits its mimetic function, but also its shock value, reflecting not merely the disenfranchisement of the intellectual but the alienation of consciousness itself. It is a perspective achieved not through the imposition of false values, but by a continuous process of devaluation which can only finally encounter *Adiaphora* — matters of indifference.

In its unquestioning acceptance of Modernist assumptions of innovation and novelty rather than truthfulness to experience, Textualism adopts the platitudinous superiority of the Avant-Garde, trading in the sanctity of critical distance for a heroic individualism, no less pious, and no less pathetic than that of the most pretentious artist — with a resulting vocabulary no less subjective and even more obscure than the "Bourgeois" criticism it affects to oppose.

11. The Anxiety of Non-Influence

The scientists were saying that by science Man was learning more and more about himself as an organism, and more and more about the world as an environment, and that accordingly the environment could be changed and man made to feel more and more at home. The Humanists were saying that by the application of ethical principles of Christianity man's lot was certain to improve. But the poets and artists and novelists were saying something else: that at a time when according to the theory of the age, men should feel most at home, they felt most homeless.

—Walker Percy

One of the most fashionable contemporary critical theories involves a highly exaggerated notion of the necessity for the Artist to rid himself of his progenitors — a Freudian version of Marx's nightmare of history weighing upon all generations. The broad appeal of this Oedipal fantasy can only be explained by the fact that it is so satisfying in the graduate school environment, vindicating generational aggression. By inflating the agonistic drama of the artist, the fantasy tends to erase his concrete accomplishments — only the most recent example of the intelligentsia absorbing art.

Let us hypothesize that with Post-Modernism we are dealing with a literature *without* primary influences, and for that matter, without satisfying primordial combat. First of all, if there is an obsession with paternalistic influence, it is above all directed at the "Second Revolution," and so we are dealing with a surrogate father at best. Secondly, there is little evidence that there has been much active repudiation of the dominant native strain of American fiction — the Hemingway/Fitzgerald/Faulkner axis. American fiction simply turned its back on these influences with some diffidence during the fifties, and there has been no powerful inclination to return. The Post-Modern implies a literature which lacks a known parenthood. Whether this is a salutary event is not the point here; but certainly American writers of the last thirty years have been more influenced by literatures in other languages and non-literary disciplines than their immediate forebears, and their reaction has more often than not been one of pragmatic and selective assimilation rather than emulation/patricide. To this extent, Post-Modernism opposes the nationalist literary traditions institutionalized by the Academy, as well as the reductive filial relationships they presuppose. There is no father, dead or alive; and that, of course, constitutes a complex of a special kind.

However the detachment from national models is ultimately accounted for, we are dealing with a movement of inner proliferation rather than a reaction against authority. It may well be that we are worse off without the hostility to previous generations which gave a sense of significance and continuity to literary combat, but to see recent literary history as a bitter struggle, subliminal or otherwise, with cultural authoritarianism is simply wishful thinking.

The most salient fact about the literary innovation of the last thirty years is that it has had such little effect upon the critical establishment. If this was a revolution, it was a revolution with no counter-reaction whatsoever. Inflation mutes confrontation. We lack, unfortunately or no, any direct dialectical relationship with our immediate historical precursors, *or* between contemporaneous writers and critics. We are dealing with the anxiety of *non*-influence.

* * * *

The irrelevance of precursors is most notable in contemporary fiction, for the genre of the novel, unlike any other, carries within it a caricatural twin — the entertainment novel — which is essentially empty but formally indistinguishable from its literary counterpart. It is one thing to escape one's influences, quite another to have as an ongoing strategy the differentiation of one's efforts from a common but inferior denominator. Any serious contemporary fiction sets out with a vengeance to be unlike those books it disparages. Even beginning writers now start by *parodying* rather than *imitating*. In an effort to ironize the entertainment novel or the "classic," they aim to create a diametrically opposed work which builds its identity not upon the wreckage of something it has destroyed, but against the very formulaic success of its twin. This accounts for the triumph of *counter-genre* as a self-conscious repudiation of coextensive literary dreck. The *counter-genre* has become the dominant formula of our time. Conventional Genre is as much the enemy as the Genteel ever was.

All this is to say that you can overkill any idea, even as good a one as wrenching fiction from its journalistic origins, from what Pound called the "Clog of the Mimetic." Despite fiction's movement, as Woolf predicted, towards an abstract world once associated exclusively with poetry, it must always contend with and contest the muddy Mississippi of its popular counterpart, which is to say that generically speaking it cannot deflect conventional reality entirely, nor can it totally empty itself, as hard as it tries, of the banality of meaning. In fiction, there is always an *excess* of meaning which is not voluntary. Painting can become autonomous by changing its theory of geometry; fiction cannot so fundamentally deny its interaction with its generic environment. The result of setting out to divest literature of its philosophical burden often produces extremely tendentious and programmatically philosophical books. There may not be much in the way of ideas in the *noveau roman*, but there is a stifling aura of jettisoned ideas. The excessive pleading for advanced cognition often reduces the novel to the discovery of new forms, in the process ignoring the fact that we are dealing with a genre which derives much of its strength from processes not strictly linguistic. John Fowles confronts the question directly: "to what extent am I being a coward by writing inside the old tradition? To what extent am I being panicked into avant-gardism?"

To understand the phenomenon of *counter-genre*, we must emphasize the gap between various literary forms and their legendaric terminology. David Grossvogel exemplifies the convoluted pattern:

> The writer who finds the intent of his fiction so jeopardized may try as an initial tactic to frustrate the alienating drift of critical speculation by making a propitiatory offering of his own being . . . admitting in advance of the reader that his fiction is mere pattern — a recognizably fraudulent object. . . . When the novel can no longer tell a simple tale, it becomes the mode that notes the indifference of its reader and finds the new dimensions of its fiction in the relation of that reader to the author through the object between them. *[Limits of the Novel]*

The counter-genre is essentially a *deflationary* medium, reacting initially against the romance, its ogres and maidens, and in the present era against the pretensions of the High Modernism. As Realism burlesqued Romance, as the Bourgeois came to receive ironic treatment in the Bourgeois novel, so the Post-Modernist subjects the Modernists' exclusive emphasis on the protean to parody, ironizing the conventions of fragmentation, simultaneity, and formlessness without end, attacking the dogma of individualized style. But just as the critical languages of the Second Revolution tend to cancel one another out, so the counter-genre is also attenuated as it becomes increasingly formulaic. Irony is no longer, in J.A.K. Thompson's words, "a trembling equipoise between jest and earnest," but a series of reductions in stature.

Once others' aesthetic claims are fully ironized, the only thing the artist has left to undercut are his *own* claims to authority — an enterprise in which the culture will prove a most willing partner.

12. In the Wake of the Wake

The object of the novelist is to keep the reader entirely oblivious of the fact that the author exists — even of the fact he is reading a book.

—*Ford Madox Ford*

Effecting a siege without an enemy, contemporary fiction defensively attempts to reassert its old imperatives, but without mimetic pretensions. This produces not so much the imperial novel, but a full appropriation of a verbal universe which one might uncharitably call hysterification, or the overwrought novel — what we will call *absolutist fiction*.

Nevertheless, it is epistemologically as absurd to think that one can create a novel from words alone as it is to suppose that one can journalistically slice up a life and pass it off as a triumph of the imagination. It is also psychologically absurd to think of a work of art as completely self-contained. Fiction is always in a primary sense derivative, reciprocally evocative in spite of itself. Whatever one imagines one has added to creation, one is only giving back in contrived form what one has already received.

But it is nevertheless the strategy of many Post-Modern works to memorialize in every sentence that what is going on *is* filtered, the product of a sensibility which requires *your* duration; indeed it is the central premise of such work constantly to remind you, lest you have somehow forgotten, just who is in charge. This is quite different from the traditional omniscient narrator, who, through his pro-forma power effectively makes the reader forget he is being manipulated — the amnesia we call "getting swept up in the story." While such novels appeal to the exegetical mind, they disclaim external evidence, eschew the reciprocal, the reportorial, the historical, and at times even the felt — but all with a prodigious verbal activity which insists that they are *creating* everything they tell us.

Obvious recent examples would be Barth's *Letters*, Coover's *The Public Burning*, Gaddis's *J.R.*, McElroy's *Lookout Cartridge* and Pynchon's *Gravity's Rainbow* (to choose the extremely frustrated efforts of extremely talented people). Even Norman Mailer has recently tried his hand at it in *Ancient Evenings*, and there are no doubt more to come. Such books possess a *complexity of surface*, a kind of verbal hermetic seal which holds them together, irrespective of linear pattern or narrative momentum. They lack both the depth and momentum which we associate with traditional narratives, but their *verbal* density gives them weight and palpability. While they may fail to give consistent pleasure, they are sophisticated precisely because they function very much like the primitive brain, eschewing every familiar sentiment and facility of absorption. They are absolutist in their insistence that objective reference is not merely impossible, but irrelevant. It is always wrong to apply painterly terms to literature, but it must be said that if there is a true Abstract Expressionism in American literary art, it can be found most palpably in the extravagant and aesthetically utopian prose fiction of the last decade, which insists that literature ought to be appreciated for the *elements of its composition;* an arrangement in which the possibility of *any* parallel reality is usurped not by the veracity but the voracity of language. However these efforts are ultimately judged, the form of such fiction is what used to be called content.

The problem, of course, is that even the most intelligent reader resists such books, which continue nevertheless to come at us as if objections were irrelevant. Here it is useful to consider the imperialism of a new Managerial class, the tendency to disregard the resistance of traditional phenomena, to overmanage — based on a belief that technological innovation can free itself from history, a tinkering which nevertheless requires large theories to defend it. It was these writers' political and intellectual contemporaries, after all, who believed for the first time in history that you could fine tune and smooth out the natural fluctuations of the business cycle, which heretofore no one thought subject to human control; that a limitless supply of organizational techniques would automatically result in steady growth and increased productivity. The idea is, that if you could get the novel to *work better*, to *work harder*, to work at full capacity, as it were, then everything else would take care of itself. The effect of this utopianism, untempered by experience or circumstance, in art no less than the economy, is of course an inflation which the controlling intelligence of technique alone is powerless to reverse. It ultimately runs up hard against its own self-generated limits, unreasonable if understandable expectations struck down by conventional wisdom. This accounts for our response to these books, for inflation starts out looking too good to be true, a perpetual motion machine without raw materials or markets. But as the plot progresses, we come to notice that *it's as good as it's going to get*; and so for the first time in the history of literature we respond with a version of: "It's terrific. But I wish it were over." We are thus surrounded by unfinished masterpieces — unfinished by the reader. He is put off not by the length or depth, but by an *attitude* of the writer who insists upon revealing not his resolution, but his determinants. Consciousness does not progress infinitely any more than profits, productivity, or moral betterment. An advance in cognition is not necessarily an epistemological advance. A wisdom based solely upon technical leverage, no matter how ingenious, is not sustainable without irrational anticipation by its consumer. Absolutism ignores the existence of natural obstacles at its peril, and thus cannot lend itself to maturation, in either the works themselves or the careers they imply.

This impulse does not, incidentally, leave the reader out of the literary equation. In fact what these books presuppose is the cooperation of an *ideal* reader, an elite which will preserve new works until they come to constitute a real canon beyond category. And there is nothing so naive in this view as the assumption that the Academy, even more susceptible to changes in fashion than the commercial world, will provide this function. The one thing we know for certain about Post-Modernism is that it will *not* be followed by an enthusiastic army of second generation interpreters.

These are perhaps the first works consciously written, not for posterity — but *only* for posterity — a true future fiction for an audience which not only does not exist, but *cannot* exist unless it progresses with the same utopian technical advancement of expertise, the same accelerating value, which informs the verbal dynamic of the novels written for them. This represents an act of ultimate aggression against the contemporary audience.

The *cul de sac* of such an enterprise is illustrated by William Burroughs' division of narrative into three parallel columns, which, in mimicking the newspaper, presumably replicates a reality which operates simultaneously on multiple tracks. The problem is of course that even the most advanced Evelyn Wood student could not read the columns simultaneously, so the aesthetic presumption of a tripled peripheral perception is defeated by the *physiological* limitations of the reader. We may have a literary landscape featuring only fragments, but we nevertheless still experience those fragments in a linear fashion and more or less one at a time, even if our attention is "creatively" divided. In other words, this is an aesthetic experience recommended for a species which has yet to appear on earth.

As should be clear by now, mine is not an argument for moderation. If compromise is what we are after, there is after all a *species* of Post-Modernism which is identifiable as historical realism patinaed with the "special effects" of Modernism — journalistic portraiture updated by ironical caveat, cinematic fragmentation, and didactic narration, whose market code word is the "accessible serious," and whose primary effect is a kind of double nostalgia both for absorbed Modernist innovation *and* 19th century narration. Doctorow's *Ragtime*, Irving's *Hotel New Hampshire*, and Thomas's *White Hotel* are recent examples, and the paucity of this compromise is underlined by the fact that these novelists all write much better when they don't try to have it both ways.

The most obvious example of our ongoing humiliation, however, is the recent reaction against the experiment, a fashionable Neo-Realism, which through its willful underdeployment of resources, its mirror image of the most questionable features of Absolutism, comes to constitute the deflationary mode of Literal Revivalism. It is the classic conservative response to inflation — underutilization of capacity, reduction of inventory, and verbal joblessness. This is not the minimalism of Barthelme, whose omissions are based on the circumspect demonstration that he *knows* what he is leaving out. These are the elisions of inadvertency and circumscription, an obdurate unsurprised and unsurprising plainstyle which takes that famous "meaning between the lines" to its absurd conclusion, and makes the middle ground mimesis of an Updike or Cheever seem rococo by comparison. (Ann Beattie and Raymond Carver are the obvious aristocracy of this genre.)

Against the exploitative chaos of Absolutism, its spurious complexity and contradiction, an addiction which subverts an author's maturity, a supermannerism which cannot be sustained, we get in this Neo-

Realism a funky tranquility which poses as a spurious objectivity, a simplemindedness based on the false innocence of forms, an artless analgesic worse than the addiction, and the refusal to allow any aspect of *literariness* to sharpen or develop, much less progress. It memorializes the hard won dead end Absolutism has brought us to — without knowing it.

Against a pathological proteanism which dissipates its power, we get a passivity which refuses reflection. Against the fever of the subversive, we get a low grade infection of the banal. Against the mindless misappropriation of the metaphors of modern science, we get the concrete in the form of tennis shoes and the mandatory beer poured over the head. Against a cost overrun linguistics, we get rent-controlled vernacular. Against the acronym, oxymoron and farcically symbolic names, we get brand names, first names, and nicknames. Against the congested cloverleaf of space/time warp, we get a withered first person present as straight and endless as a Nebraska thruway. Against the tyranny of originality, we get the story as mass produced and interchangeable part. Against the refusal to convince and represent, we get the self-evident which is never demonstrated. Against the airless self-referential, we get the singular claustrophobia of place. Against the hysterical rantings of over-verbalized abstractions, we get the drama of the spacey domestic in reduced emotional circumstances. Against the author whom we would like to throttle, we get characters who we can only hope we'll never meet again. Against the zany overblown disembodied voices we could never trust, we get a "real people" narrator whose trust is restored at the price of our interest in him. Against a profligate wisdom pissed away in endless interrogation, we get stupidity and dullness passed off as indigenous American virtues. Against Grandiose Hyperbole, we get the Sententious Laconic. For arch complicity, the humble sly. For logorrhea, a logo.

> Susan combs her hair. She leaves her black mittens on, and Charles thinks that she looks like some weird animal with big paws. She's a nice sister. He wishes he could think of something to do with her.
>
> "If you stop at a store, I'll buy something to fix for dinner," she says.
>
> "You feel like fixing dinner?"
>
> She shrugs. Laura likes to cook. Laura and the Ox are probably eating a late dinner together in their cold A-frame. Tomorrow

he will see Laura. Laura's hair is longer than Susan's, Laura wears perfume. She wears *Vol de Nuit*. She gives *Vol de Nuit* to Jim's first wife for a present . . . .

[Ann Beattie, *Chilly Scenes of Winter*]

If you don't care for *entropicalamity in excelsis*, how's about a whiff of *Vol de Nuit*?

This pronounced division of labor, a kind of static double helix, in which the velocity of two rotating aesthetic traditions shorn of historical context simultaneously cancel each other out, testifying to the absence of any experience strong enough to modify habits of mind, could only happen in Post-Modern America.

13. The End Game Strategy

The important point I tried to argue with Henry James was that the novel of completely consistent characterization, arranged beautifully in a story and painted deep, round and solid, no more exhausts the possibilities of the novel than the art of Velásquez exhausts the possibilities of the painted picture.

—H.G. Wells

Absolutist fiction in its extreme Formalism may be as dubious as it is ambitious, but we should recall that fiction always exists in a double sense: as reports on changing patterns of human behavior, as well as on the evolution of forms. Modernism held out the hope that while industrialism and science were increasingly out of control, we could nevertheless through art create an edifice of the imagination appropriate to a scientific age. Once we began to query our aesthetic means and materials, however, questioning them as much as the world, then the mythology of art as compensation would no longer do. To exemplify — as absolutist fiction does — the problematical nature of art demeans neither the artist nor his function, but simply unburdens literature from having to function as a secular religion, an illusory preserve within the ravages of technology and the absurdity of our politics. To agree that art alone cannot give a complete image of man's self is potentially to reaffirm both the richness of our humanity and the possibilities of artistic enterprise. In an age when we have, at the same moment, dismissed both our utopian notions of the future and any continuity with the past, the new mythology is that we have none. "I have killed the last myth" — that is the narrative imposture of our times. Yet it is not an entirely inappropriate aesthetic strategy. Literature is not religion, or philosophy, or psychology, it is not a political act, or intrinsically virtuous, neither weapon nor sanctuary; least of all is it therapy. Literature attends primarily to worn-out metaphors, faded vocabularies of self-description, and we are just beginning to discover that these vocabularies are not national treasures or even genre properties.

While retracting earlier claims for literature may be to some extent self-cancelling (and not a little self-righteous), it is not, on the whole, self-deceptive. For those writers and critics who would write off writing with writing, who proclaim the terminus of language, are in fact making, however obliquely, the highest claims for their own use of it. [The language is dead. Long live my lingo!] The same gesture which proclaims the extinction of the language animal affirms the power of the writer's own speech, and this is a paradox which is finally, even at times marvelously, unassimilable. In this situation, it is of distinct benefit to adopt the pose of the Last Artist, to play dead, to have, in fancy, *the last word*.

And while the tone of much of this literature is both self-parodic and contemptuous of the reader, its very limitations often intensify its claim on our attention. For the presumption here is roughly this: that, for better or worse, language is our first and primary human institution. The recovery of our primordial origins is no more possible than any projected utopia of undifferentiated consciousness; and literature, insofar as it challenges the established language of the moment, may be understood as a basic survival mechanism rather than a form of transcendence. Language is a *given*, a phenomenon which is neither autonomous *nor* coextensive with our lives. And literature, thus, is a gift — not the property of a class or even an individual prophet — a present, which, like all exemplary endowments, creates its own terms of acceptance. This view of literature, although stripped of the older sanctions of High Art, nevertheless reasserts in a hardheaded way the primacy of language as a reorientive enterprise, and in so doing proclaims the continuity of the Modernist impulse by taking its assumptions to logical if unsettling conclusions.

A matter of Tactics, remember. If one poses as the "last" writer, if one writes the "last" novel, one is also the beginning as well. One has one's tale firmly in one's mouth. Being last, after all, is a good way to be first and a good way of being visible. Also, posing as terminal redirects our attention, by sleight of hand, to how we *became* — reinventing history by tearing it from encrusted genre and stale metaphor.

Fiction has become a vehicle for the disparate voices of the intellect and verbal innovation rather than a story-telling machine. It has come to rely upon its own linguistic awareness of itself, rather than plot or character development, to provide its momentum. But at the very moment we have begun to understand the legitimacy of the self-reflexive, the impulse seems to be waning; the age of involution is already past. Barthelme is, after all, the most imitated writer in the country today — fully as much as Salinger and Hemingway once were. (One index of genius is the extent to which it prompts redundancy in lesser talents.)

Nevertheless, our best known critics — our most recent last men of letters — have preferred to be dismissive of their contemporaries. Such a lack of continuity is also certified by the Realist Revivalists — of whom Bellow has been the most vocal — whose literary sensibility is so threatened by youth culture and its nonverbal strategies that they cannot see how pitiable and transient these gestures are, nor how much, in fact, they owe to their vitalistic predecessors. And so these "Realists" too "play dead," insist that *they* are the end of things, that their notion of received meaning represents the culmination of Modernism, their accomplishment the final repository of significant and acute value.

After all, what is "exhausted" is not literature, but its market. Its terms are defined not by the writer withholding his bid, but when the last buyer has executed his final buy. The "last reader" is a far more interesting metaphor than any latest "last writer." Just as Modernism made it impossible for us passively to glean answers to moral questions from literature, Post-Modernism destroys the belief that aesthetic evolution alone can definitively alter our perception. Confronted with an audience which through the ministrations of the Second Revolution has discounted in advance all possibility of being shocked, it is the writer who is often left holding the toxic bag of his latest *catastrophisme*. His aggressiveness is in direct proportion to the coolness of his audience.

Contemporary writing exists uneasily between an establishment which sees *Finnegans Wake* as the end of a genre, or a beginning, and an adolescent culture which sees itself as somehow sprung fully armed from the void: "we are the *other* people — nuthin' like us *ever* was!"

Clearly we have a considerable body of fiction which exemplifies new possibilities for narrative as for the entire aesthetic enterprise itself, writing which cannot be explained by reference to Modernist masters or assimilated by a literary culture still ruled by Modernist assumptions. But just as clearly, most claims for a "new sensibility" seem perversely ahistorical and obscurantist, merely deflecting whatever genuine claims might be made for contemporary writing. It is very American that the young should see themselves with no antecedents, but it is more surprising that established critics and writers see themselves without contemporary consequences. If we have changed so much, then never has a major mutation been absorbed so quickly or described so sloppily. More likely, our extreme rhetoric both energizes and masks whatever significant change is occurring. And if we can only really understand what is happening to us by watching ourselves describe it, then the strategy of dying, of feigned exhaustion, again reasserts a tactical urgency. For by posing as *last*, a culmination in an age which views itself as *a*historical, you gain attention, if not affection, from those who can only see themselves as specialists in the new, and who are forever yet to be. The End Game Strategy, though by now tedious in the extreme, may prove in retrospect to have been necessary to open up the game again.

14. Neo-Conservatism and the Unrevolutionization of Literature

Strictly speaking . . . readers aren't what they used to be . . . so being a writer isn't what it used to be. But the demands of art are the same.

—*J. F. Powers*

To the extent that Absolutist Fiction is abstract, it is problematic. To the extent that it is problematic, it risks indifference. To the extent that it takes that risk, it is highly defensive in stance. Such defensiveness is not simply some Nietzschean effluvium settled in the century's craw, but a social fact exacerbated over the last two decades by an increasingly shrill series of intellectually vengeful attacks upon the literary, particularly the fictional transaction itself.

Recall, for example, the recent avalanche of critical speculations which have assigned literature to the marginal. One may as well begin with Norman Podhoretz's claim that the "best and brightest" should switch to the documentary essay as the only suitable way to analyze society's problems. Tom Wolfe upped the ante with the "new journalism" as replacement for a fatigued fiction. (Curious that journalism now increasingly encroaches upon the precincts of fiction, the oldest plagiary.) Talese claimed his characters were better than imagined ones because you could call them up on the telephone. Roth proclaimed American society so bizarre it was impossible for any fiction to equal it. Howe dismissed the contemporary as Avant-Garde *manqué*. Barzun sang a requiem for high art, while Trilling was merely diffident. Youth culture offed literature as the dying privatized irrelevancy of a privileged class, only codifying existing forms of establishment power, inviting cultural repression, paternalism and elitism. Bellow mourned the passing of standards and the unwillingness of the Establishment to do its severe and obvious duty. Marcuse granted to art only a negating quality. Laing and Brown saw literary activity as hopelessly anal, repressive as well as sublimative, and an entire generation of analects asserted that language as differentiation bears no necessary correspondence to reality, with the ultimate result that any truth claim made by art was simply another non-claim — throwing out significance itself with the mimetic bath water. It was of course McLuhan who provided the *coup de grâce* by suggesting that the poor "print-oriented bastards" had been locked into the wrong technology.

There was, of course, also simple fatigue. Joseph Epstein writes the epitaph of a man whose library has failed him:

> . . . as the years go by, he finds himself reading less and less fiction, or more precisely contemporary fiction. The big-ticket items [sic] . . . he does read. . . .
>
> The story itself has indubitably lost ground, probably since Joyce; and since Joyce, too, it can probably be said that most fiction divides itself betwixt that which relies on style and that which relies on story — though the two need not be always compatible — with those that rely on story being, I should say, better . . . ["Is Fiction Necessary?"]

Is it any wonder that writers might be put on the defensive by such a chorus of intellectual negations? The single most damaging blow to fiction is its lack of intellectual *cachet*, for an audience which has been reduced to intellectuals. At any rate, we have not heard very much recently about the ability of the literary imagination to illuminate history and social fact, challenge our complacency, force us to recognize the distance between values and acts; never mind the business about the enduring and prevailing of man.

We are faced with a curious syndrome here. Contemporary literature tends to browbeat the passive general reader while being browbeaten in turn by an intellectual class which finds fiction an insufficient weapon for cultural analysis. The fact of the matter is that the middle distance strategy of fictional narrative cannot satisfy claims for Hard News any more than for True Mysticism. It cannot transcend its hybrid origins, nor should it try. It is by now a cliché that literature, and American literature in particular, has defaulted upon concrete social analysis, the interaction of character and milieux. But can it really be said that our fictions offer less congruence with reality than the paradigms offered by behaviorism in sociology, functionalism in political science, positivism in philosophy, monetarism in economics, pop/camp in painting, or structuralism in literary studies? No, what they all hold in common is their marvelous autonomy, which amounts by this time to nothing more than the abandoning of hope of affecting any larger public polity. Autonomy in inflation adds up to nothing more than a process of progressive self-disenfranchisement.

The most interesting thing about the various theories is that while they begin by questioning the potential of fiction for social truth, they end with a common attempt to liberate the mind from the albatross of western rationalism. From this one would expect an onrush of uncoopted sentiment; but rarely, if ever, has an attack on cerebration been so cerebral, rarely has a plan for the reunification of the senses been couched in so antiseptic a form. Unable to establish a romantic alternative to scholastic analysis, the Post-Modern critical intellect often finds it sufficient simply to subvert art.

Nowhere is this better illustrated than in the more than cursory relationship between the old Liberalism and the new Formalism, as well as between Neo-Conservatism and Literal Revivalism. For the Neo-Conservative attacks the Post-Modernist with a vehemence which only two rival inauthentic neologisms could engender, and what we often end up with is a contest between the passively malignant and the gratuitously vicious. Indeed the contemporary realist/formalist debate lacks symmetry because the associated political terminology has become so meaningless. It is confusing enough to divide writers into realists and non-realists; to assign them positions on the right and left, respectively, is totally to trivialize the debate. There could be no art less political, much less "leftist," than contemporary formalism, and those Americans who purport to take their leftist ideology seriously are invariably conservative, if not totally reactionary in their aesthetic techniques.

Nevertheless, the most discouraging feature of contemporary intellectual life is not the continuing irrelevance of orthodox leftist pieties, but the failure of the Neo-Conservative revisionism to offer any alternative to the Modernist canon. For Post-Modernist irony and deflection require straightmen who defend realism — and to the extent that tradition has become cowed, to the extent Modernism has lacked adventitious obstacles, it comes to reflect those maladies associated with an excess of strength, becoming itself inflexible and breaking up into an immense contingency.

The Neo-Conservative critique goes something like this: Classic Modernism is our only vital tradition, but it has been subverted not only by its success, but by the institutionalized acceptance of an Anarcho-Leftist sensibility which programmatically disassociates itself from the culture's basic values while accepting its blandishments. Such an "adversary" culture continues to titillate society — though with neither the *élan* nor *écart* of High Modernism — and to politicize art without taking responsibility for its actions. Particularly to be scorned is the Socialist who evinces an interest in popular culture, since he renounces simultaneously the political values of mainstream society as well as the aesthetics of High Modernist culture. It is preposterous for intellectuals to complain about a system which has provided a secure haven from totalitarianism as well as an unprecedented standard of living for intellectuals as a class. The American intellectual/artist is essentially a spoiled brat, and critical standards have been fatefully eroded by his posturings.

There is nothing much wrong with this as an ideological gloss, and it exposes the most unattractive feature of Post-Modernist culture — that conspicuous lack of gratitude for *anything*, which parades as "cool" but masks a singular lack of courage. Modernism could survive the destruction of European society, but not the retrogressive embrace of American culture. We tend to forget that brief flush of enthusiasm — so different from the initial European appropriation of Modernism — that uniquely American projection of a large-spirited, full-handed, and even beneficent culture; one which never really got off the ground. Recall that when the Museum of Modern Art moved into its present quarters in 1939, its inventory was collected not from Bohemian *ateliers* but from the basement of the *Time-Life* Building, and that the President of the Republic himself could welcome this event in a radio address:

> In encouraging the creation and enjoyment of beautiful things,
> we are furthering democracy itself . . .

No politician would claim such cause and effect today.

There is even less reciprocity between language and power than between "beauty" and "democracy." In the 1950's when the C.I.A.

was establishing close links with publishing houses, the head of its covert action staff could testify before the Church committee:

> Books differ from all other propaganda media, because one single book can significantly change the reader's attitude and action to an extent unmatched by any other medium . . . books are the most important weapon of strategic propaganda . . .

No one believes that print culture retains such power, much less that literary modernism might be an effective weapon in cold war or any other politics.

The Neo-Conservative critique ignores the extent to which Modernism played itself out through its own institutionalized success; it also exaggerates the Post-Modern reaction, which in fact collapses from its own weightlessness. It sidesteps the possibility that Post-Modernism might be understood as a peculiar amalgam of high *and* popular culture, which does not find its place either in habitual adversary or commercial categories, much less in those of Realism and Formalism. The Neo-Conservative makes the fatal mistake of believing that only *his* values have been threatened. Thus, he is generally intimidated by the impenitent humor of the era, baffled by those who seem to take pride in being cheerful historians of collapse — testimony only to the fact that the moral conscience of Modernism cannot be restored by solemnity or scolding.

As with all 20th century ideologies, the Neo-Conservative brings forth a new "realism" with which to attack a decadent "formalism," but it is a realism in this case which has fully absorbed the Modernist canon. Nevertheless, every writer, as Robbe-Grillet says, "thinks he is a realist," and it is a little late (and requires little courage) to call the Avant-Garde's bluff, as they themselves have for some time managed their own self-destruction quite as well as the bourgeoisie before them. As the Avant-Garde kept twitting the bourgeois of the Fifties for thirty years, the Neo-Conservative generation apparently cannot give up its obsession with the Avant-Garde of the Sixties, reflecting the American preference for the *vanished* enemy. The myth of the doomed creative artist fighting the smug philistine has been replaced by the myth of the parasitical artist living off the public trust. This, alas, is as far as we have managed to come.

In fact, the Neo-Conservative offers only a penultimate version of the Avant-Garde/Bourgeois drama. The vanguard is scorned to the extent that he exploits the bourgeois, but the bourgeois is redeemed to the extent that he absorbs the vanguard. Bourgeois is no longer bad — *to the degree that he adopts Modernism*. Any concession to Pre- or Post-Modernist art smacks of apostasy.

This lack of skepticism regarding Modernism is really the most astonishing thing about Neo-Conservatism. Partly it reflects the conservative fascination with technology and science, partly it is an effort to overcome the "old fogey" image of its own right wing, the fear of being "out of date" which mirrors the intimidation of genteel liberals by their own left wing — a contest of harping on what is new to the extent that they both lose touch with what is continuous.* Whatever the case, there has been a notable effort to link Neo-Conservative politics with Modernist culture, under the rubric of indigenous Americanism. Attend to Jeffrey Hart, speaking to his *National Review* audience:

> The average American is a modernist in his bones. Americans believe in possibility, in "making it new," as Ezra Pound once urged. If conservatism is to be truly American, it must embrace that sense of possibility. We like to say that conservatism is the politics of reality. Well, that is the cultural reality. A truly popular American conservatism must be modern, because most Americans are modern. They do not live on ducal estates. They don't even go to Groton. And because they are modernizers they are also anti-Communists . . . The modern artist is concerned to assert his freedom, and that involves an adversary relationship to past conventions . . . a modern work creates its own conventions . . . If you look at other areas of life, you will see immediately that freedom advances inexorably . . . We must learn to live amidst discontinuities, whose discontinuousness is transcended only by love. Art has entirely separated itself from morality, even from "content" as traditionally understood. The Newtonian universe is gone. The universe is a mathematical equation. The holistic world view expressed in natural law is fading; at the very least, the "natural law" will have to be reformulated.

*It is fascinating to ponder how Modernism in America provided a home for groups as diverse as the Jewish immigrant intelligentsia (who saw in it revolutionary potential), and that element of the WASP Artistocracy who saw it as civilizing and conservatory. They are together now, in the retirement condominium of the axial Foundation/University/Museum world, which was not, presumably, their heart's desire.

This breezy formulation, indistinguishable from the prattle of any left-wing Modernist Manqué, so ahistorical, so uncritical, so *unconservative* in its bland acceptance of an art detached from all other values, only reinforces Trilling's major insight that we have always lacked a flourishing conservative intellectual tradition to refine a vaguely liberal modernism. In any other context, the conservative would have marshalled an argument against the *homo aestheticus* of a self-contained Modernist utopianism, rather than breathlessly testifying to the fact that High Modernism has become the ruling culture of the Haut-Bourgeoisie. "No artist of any kind," T.S. Eliot reminds us, "has his complete meaning alone . . . tradition cannot be inherited; if you want it, you must attain it by great labor . . . the historical sense has a simultaneous existence and composes a simultaneous order."

Like the Avant-Garde before it, Neo-Conservatism is a narrow and immature interpretation of its own grand tradition — which is to say, rather than bringing forth the past to grant the future a perspective, it brings forth the recently canonized past to attack the overly categorized present, pausing only to occasionally "draw the line" as Kenner does with Faulkner, or Epstein with Joyce. Perhaps an ahistorical conservatism is what an ahistorical liberalism deserves.

The Neo-Conservative aesthetic is confused, for it is at once curatorial in its bland acceptance of Modernism, and populist in indifference to the effects of technology. On the one hand it attacks the mass media for glorifying violence, for its lack of cohesive spiritual and social values; on the other it defends an unrestricted acquisitiveness as the ruling social passion, a "free" market which functions precisely because it is devoid of values. The unsolved confusion of the Neo-Conservative intellectual is that while he professes to despise mass culture (and the "liberal" media which propagate it) he defends to the death the socio-economic system which insures its hegemony. He simply refuses to recognize the enormous disproportion (contradiction would be too dignified) between the multiformity of American art, the protean nature of American social life, and the unprecedented power of the "market maker" in the culture. It is no wonder that this invariably results in a highly sublimated personality.

Moreover, if the Avant-Garde is wedded to a sclerotic Socialism or pseudo-Anarchism, the Neo-Conservative argument is self-limiting by its conventional economic liberalism. If the Avant-Garde requires a coherent enemy, the conservative needs something to defend. So while it is perfectly appropriate to ridicule the radical who takes refuge in non-profit institutions, the conservative is stuck with the achievements of the vaunted private sector, and the not so invisible fist of the self-regulating "free market." The continuing problem of credibility for the cultural Neo-Conservative is that he can postulate no alternative to the commercial free market, which in the case of the communications industry cannot be said to be distorted by "Leftist" covert political action or economic welfarism. If the Neo-Conservative is to offer anything beyond a redistribution of wealth to the affluent, he must question the hegemony of Modernism, those secularized, cerebrized and distorted perceptions which take such a grossly individuated form (culture as aesthetic swindle). The achilles heel of the Neo-Conservative is not his quaint faith in a rawer capitalism, but his excessively pious acceptance of Modernism, the failure to ask that art be accountable and not simply another self-justifying enterprise detached from all other values. What is to be chalked up against this conservatism is that in its confusion of a free-market of commodities with a stock exchange of received ideas, it exerts in culture, no less than in foreign policy, a profoundly destabilizing force — refusing the test of its own tradition, which is the restoration of faith in institutions.

As for the "private sector," that euphemism for deregulated oligopoly, it is difficult to see how cultural resources would be allocated more effectively by a corporate vice president for public affairs than a government bureaucrat, and given the fact that corporate gifts result in a massive loss of tax revenues, it is doubtful they are even cost-effective. If there is to be a new ethical force marshalled against social and cultural disintegration, it is unlikely that supply side economics will provide it. It was Adam Smith who projected a utopian state in which human activity would be totally "atomized."

This is compounded by the hypocrisy of a conservative movement which cries out for a return to the "free market" but funds its own "anti-establishment" activities through massive internal subsidy. If the Neo-Conservatives had to depend on the "free market" for the dissemination of its ideology, no one would have ever heard of them.

The Conservative tradition is, after all, supremely relevant to the present moment. For its strength has always been in producing a more historically oriented view of evolution and a more tragic and complex view of life, a world-view which emphasizes the interdependence of human and artistic limitation, the necessity for functioning institutions, and a skepticism about sacrificing human life in the service of *any* theory. Yet rather than revivifying institutions, the Neo-Conservatives have managed only to create a new "Adversary" style as shrill and ideological as that of the Anarcho-Leftism it has replaced. Rather than emphasize a consensual interdependence based upon shared sacrifice, and a conservatory discipline which would mitigate an inflationary psychology, it has aimed its appeal at yet another atomized individualism (a kind of socioeconomic formalism) which appears incommensurable in American life. It plays to a middle class whose security and identity have been eroded by inflation, justifing a self-aggrandizement without guilt, capitalizing upon the *banality of revolution*, the empty rhetoric of Avant-Garde pretensions. It is in love with authority, but can claim no authoritative figures, no heroes — with the possible exception of Russian dissidents — and is thus content simply to point out the amount of garbage that has been washed up on the beach. It offers no new standards but only a stingy pathos, that minor tonality which only echoes a dispirited Avant-Garde.

It would be mistaken to think of the recent Neo-Conservative ascendancy as a *political* victory. It is a victory, as with the New Deal before it, by default. The liberal polity simply could no longer provide a unifying context for the plural transformations within the culture. Like all liberalisms throughout the century, it was strong enough to dissolve the old political order but not strong enough to control the centrifugal cultural forces it released — particularly in an inflationary context.

But the strength of the Neo-Conservative movement should not be underestimated because the media chooses to advertise its lunatic fringe. For this is the first generation of American intellectuals since the Thirties with a will to power *beyond* their own constituency. Theirs is no liberal request for a larger share of the pie. They know the age of redistributed affluence is over. They have achieved a community to capitalize on that fact, and to effect what Trilling so distastefully referred to as "actual rule of the world."

The trappings of the "Outsider" have become as shabby as they are uniform. To their credit, Neo-Conservative intellectuals are sick and tired of being self-disenfranchised by a routine disenchantment; as a result they have made an unambivalent alliance with the new class* which has profited most from inflation.

---

*A new wealth based largely on electronics, petroleum products, government contracts, franchises, subsidies and tax write-offs, which rapidly diversified into mass communications, and promptly rationalized and legitimized the art of governmental lobbying to secure politically determined market privileges.

15. Formalist Bedrock and the Footbridge of Realism

. . . in the world as it is, there is no way to get a mastery of a subject except in the aesthetic experience . . . and if our account of it is correct, we also discover what our culture is.

—*R.P. Blackmur*

Formalism may be dead as a theory, but shorn of both its melodrama and historical context, it remains the basic underlying force in Post-Modern work. Formalism retains its operative power because in the face of mounting indifference, it holds firm in its stubborn allegiance to the intrinsically *literary,* stressing the autonomy of the language arts, which cannot be explained (or for that matter, produced) by reference to philosophical content, biographical sources, or a single technique or psychological impulse. It stresses above all the multiplicity of literary experience, and the necessity of breaking up deadening and mechanical habits—in this sense, it is most congenial to an age which lacks a period style.

Moreover, the undeniable attraction of Formalism lies in its self-appointed ideal reader, a claim given increased significance in a culture dominated by Mass Communications and its passive audience. After all, what more could a writer want than a reader who could not care less about his actual history, or the history of his composition, his psychology or his market standing, who believes that form and content are inseparable, who does not shrink from confusion, yet who assumes you mean what you say? *A reader who theoretically excludes all the uncontrollable elements of reality is irresistible*; and while Post-Modernists may not even know what Formalism is, they are invariably writing for Formalists. The irony (what else) is that while the original Formalist impulse was willfully to isolate the specifically literary for

its own good, such isolation has become in our time merely a dreary
fact of life.

This does not take into account, however, why the arguments *against*
Formalism are so weak. For if Post-Modernism is to have any lasting
influence, it is in the perception that while technique influences and
at times even entirely transforms content, the question cannot be simply
left there without severe aesthetic and psychological inertia. Trotsky
is untypically wonderful on this point.

> Please write about anything you can think of . . . ! The form of
> art is, to a certain and very large degree, independent, but the
> artist who creates form, and the spectator who is enjoying it, are
> not empty machines, one for creating form and the other for
> appreciating it. *[Literature and Revolution]*

Formalism acquires a second life in a mass culture when the
everyday language of human relations is officially banalized by the
media. Yet Formalism in its most unyielding mode also activates a
simple-minded return to Literal Revivalism: the reaction against the
experiment, the attempt to overcome autonomy by fiat.

The natural constituency for hardcore realism—the American
provincial right wing with their preference for revealed texts—literally
cannot engage Formalism, as they have been cut off from the origins
of Modernism, quite as much as their Soviet generational counterparts.
If a member of the Moral Majority were to check out his wife's reading
habits at the local library he would be less threatened if he found her
interested in William Gaddis, say, than Harold Robbins—and he would
have no idea how much trouble he was in for. Provincialism poses no
real threat to the Formalist. The extreme version of Textualist
indeterminism, that all texts are equally meaningless, is far more
damaging to literature than any Fundamentalist boobery.

The sophisticated cultural conservative, particularly one who feels
the critic's job is to draw lines rather than erase them, is in something
of a double bind. His job is to ensure the continuity of tradition, yet
the official culture of which he is presumably spokesperson is one which
programmatically celebrates discontinuity. His job is immeasurably
complicated by the lack of an authoritative figure. On the one hand,
Formalism in its methodology opens up new careers for the interpreter;
on the other, it dilutes what Tolstoy called "the transmission of
feelings" and received wisdom. While the conservative believes that art

should provide an understanding of the world beyond language, that art should be life enhancing, the lexicon by which his career is advanced remains nevertheless highly technical and linguistically grounded; he must finally resist the superstition of the word. Conventional realism simply no longer lends itself to critical attention in the same way more eccentric and experimental fictions do. Even where there is an animus towards experimental work, the conservative invariably expends his analysis upon attacking it, rather than championing any instances of contemporary realism.

It is rare that the critic attacks Formalism head on, as does Jacques Barzun:

> . . . in the contemporary arts we respond to technique, to technical innovation beyond any other appeal . . . the increasingly technical interest that our century takes in works of art means that the artist and his public meet on new ground, no longer of personality but of method. The beholder's approach is friendly and conscientious rather than passionate . . . The Interesting as an aesthetic category . . . has replaced the Beautiful, The Profound, The Moving . . . *[The Use and Abuse of Art]*

Formalism has already been forced to retreat from its own aggressive attitudinizing and bad company, as all dissenting movements must when they become routinized and when destruction by incessant novelty turns upon itself. Historically it is not infrequent that the artist comes to despise the very audience he most insisted upon.

It is no secret that Realism wanes as the idea of objective history is lost, because valid models of imitation and the continuity of certain truths require a confident historical sense. It is also clear that one does not become a Realist simply by refusing to rethink literary conventions. When John Gardner asserts that "moral art and moral criticism are necessary, and in a democracy, essential," *[On Moral Fiction]* we have a notion just as arbitrary as the one that all life is a series of fictions. But literature is no more a moral science than a natural science. The only thing we can try to do is to understand the social context of the assertion. Tolstoy's question, "What is art—if we put aside the question of beauty?" is just as apt if we substitute "Form" for Beauty—to which the Formalist would undoubtedly reply: "not much." The problem is that within Tolstoy's argument—which is Gardner's—there is not a single compelling demonstration of *how* a more moral art may be achieved, or *why* Realism contains a moral prerogative, particularly in a society characterized not so much by terror as by moral boredom. The reason is obvious: commitment of this kind cannot be formalized, despite the belief that something "real" is hidden out there. New perceptions of value can only be subsidiarily embodied in creative action; only afterwards can they be spelled out in abstract terms, which often makes them appear deliberately chosen. Moreover, the audience, so slovenly in other respects, is very quick to detect moral posturings— and it does so not by saluting references to a moral code, but by noting the artist's attitude towards his own work. Formalism may have leant itself too easily to a lazy disenchantment, but it is not countered, as in Gardner's case, by self-puffery disguised as a new sincerity. Moral realism contains its own narcissism just as surely as any aestheticism, yet another screening of commercialism behind historicist facades.

What both Tolstoy and Gardner are really talking about are theories of utility and social change—in Tolstoy's case, a high culture which was in fact built upon servitude and exploitation; in Gardner's, a society which believed for a long time that everyone had the right to beauty, that aesthetic values equalled moral values, and that what was good was good for all of us. One can only suggest that both of these notions—those of a repentant Russian nobleman, and those of an unrepentant American meliorist—have a limited currency these days, no matter how much we may regret it. We have reached a potentially dangerous situation in which very few talented people have much enthusiasm for Democracy of the spirit. Realism depends finally not so much upon a perceived continuity between the structures of art and the world, as on the belief that whether for good or ill, art is integral to a civilization, and that the artist knows whom he is dealing with, whether he approves of them or not.

One would be hard put to find any contemporary artist who believes that his best efforts will increase justice or even civility in society. The great animating idea of Liberal Progressivism has been lost in literature as it has in Post-Modern society, and to relink Realism to such notions requires more than avoiding the more psychotic and self-indulgent forms of contemporary art. It requires nothing less than a new theory of Authority, with an unblushing recognition of how Realism has been appropriated by both Statist regimes and Corporate Commercialism. Until then, we are stuck with Samuel Butler's reduction: "Art is interesting only insofar as it reveals an artist."

IV.

16. Writing Without Genre

*Is the bust of Sir Philip Crampton
epical, lyrical or dramatic?*

—*James Joyce*

The fragmentation of language and the destruction of genre are Modernism's official clichés. Its characteristic works resist classification by genre and by any anticipatory truth associated with formal conventions and patterned behavior. Genre is a way of signifying meaning in advance, and there is no concession in Modernism to an audience that wants signification in advance.

In Post-Modernism, genre continues to be botanized, subindexed (100 kinds of Formalism, 43 kinds of Impressionism), and commercial nomenclature — Health, Women, Travel, Occult, Self, Sports — may now be more efficacious categories than novel, story or poem. Marketing devices tend to reinforce the fragmentation initiated by aesthetic innovation by further segmenting the audience. As models of description, genres evolve, fade or are replaced; they blur as they resist their own taxonomy, refusing to be "common carriers." The market responds with sub-genres which recommodify consciousness. It is no accident that traditional genre fiction — gothics, mysteries, sci-fi — increases its share of the fiction market each year. Inflation increases the emphasis on the pre-*sold* commodity, which is the market's version of anticipatory truth.

To reconstitute itself, fiction often incorporates sub-genres as a matter of principle. This often results in hybrids of a certain psychological absurdity. When Norman Mailer, in *Armies of the Night*, offers "History as a Novel, the Novel as History," he is essentially disavowing the expectations and responsibilities traditionally associated with either discipline.

As genre disintegrates, the terms and the framework of the traditional contract between the author, audience, critic and reviewer are modified. As late as 1939, Virginia Woolf compared the literary situation to a London shop window, in which authors sat engaged in their work, rather like lonely seamstresses, while the audience outside watched sullenly. ["Reviewing"] It was left to the reviewers to determine which laborer's work might be worth purchasing. She goes on to complain that the distinction between the *critic* — one who deals with "past and principles" — and the *reviewer*, whose task is to inform and advertise books as they fall from the press, is no longer clear. The 19th century reviewer who emerged from the economic reorganization and professionalization of literature which took place in Goldsmith's century, reenforced by the enormous expansion of the reading public, wielded considerable power; but Woolf notes that this power was destroyed almost entirely by the *multiplicity* of reviews. It is instructive that she does not go a step further and note not only the multiplicity of *books* necessary to review, but also the emerging multiple modes of writing.

Woolf further speculated that the "reviewer's consciousness," which over two centuries had developed a formidable and not altogether unhealthy presence, coinciding with the novel's greatest period of development, no longer retained its force, and in fact had become, on the eve of the Second World War, increasingly truncated and trivial.

In such a situation, she suggested, the only hope for an author to get any genuine response was to restore the one-to-one relationship between the *true* critic and the author, a non-academic reinstitution of one of the most overrated forms of education in history, the Oxbridge tutorial: "Let the reviewers abolish themselves and resurrect themselves as doctors . . . the writer would then submit his work to the judge of his choice . . . " The quaintness of this simple relationship can hardly be surpassed. Ms. Woolf wished to smash the neat symmetry of the shop window, reinstituting a kind of pre-industrial discourse; she did not anticipate that the entire frame of reference would explode.

There is little evidence that the writer is stronger or less self-conscious in the absence of a powerful reviewing consciousness than he was. Reviewers have become "doctors" with a vengeance, and the critic's return to "first principles" — regarding literature as instances of experimental linguistics — breeds an aloofness from the work itself as well as from its potential public. As for those "tutorials," we have had in America, in the last generation, the longest ongoing pedagogic literary conversation amongst the largest number of people, in the history of mankind. No constraints of space, time, deadline or standards can be said to have obtruded upon this process, and we can hardly claim that it has produced an increase of "fearless and disinterested discussion." This is one failure that cannot be laid at the door of commercialism or mass culture. What we have witnessed, epitomized by this never ending ecumenical conversation for credit, is the double irony of an institutionalized respect for literature which disguises a diminished interest, except as transactional therapy and careerist certification. The social context and unspoken contracts of literary discourse have been modified to an extent that Woolf could not imagine; these terms are now moot.

Writing without genre is a liberating prospect, one of the few legacies of Modernism upon which the contemporary has been able to capitalize. Yet it is the fate of the Post-Modern that as the text is freed from its pre-registered status, it provides neither increased amplitude for the artist nor new access to the audience, but merely more inscriptive space for advertising and exegesis.

17. The Novelist as Poet/Critic

I am *is not a question of existence, but of grammar.*
—E.M. Cioran

It goes without saying that the novelist has encroached out of necessity upon territory once thought to be the exclusive domain of other genres. And it is clear over the past fifty years that the sentence as a synaesthetic unit can accomplish anything a line of poetry can — in terms of rhythm, heightened metaphor or metonymy — that prosody has become the province of prose, and that the structure of the contemporary novel certainly reflects more poetic internal logic than serial plotted narrative. Or to put it another way, there is not a single poetic convention or effect, including closure, which has not been reconstituted and amplified by contemporary fictional technique.

Fiction has also encroached upon criticism in its recently obsessive concern with cognitive growth. The very act of fiction now implies an act of criticism, insofar as fiction is seen as a series of transformations in modes of thinking. While poetry assumes unities which no longer exist, and criticism ponders its own aetiology, the novel struggles with its own epistemological shakiness to create an authority beyond genre, to lay grounds to be believed in, while at the same time resisting the conventional plausibility it disparages in journalism. Why poetry has traditionally attracted more systematic minds than fiction is not an easy question to answer. But it is worth remembering that no fiction writer has *ever* been able, through his own criticism, to effect a revolution of taste which would provide a home for his own work, in the tradition of a Wordsworth, Coleridge, or Eliot. This only tends to confirm the suspicion that fiction, by definition, lacks an ontology.

Just as much as criticism, fiction has become increasingly concerned with the debasement of language, and represents an assault upon the hierarchies of literary types—a coming to terms with a temporal experience which cannot be defined in advance, or dealt with in any other way. As such, it remains the riskiest of verbal endeavors, a construction which somehow must add up to something more than its steady accumulation of half-way measures, an admixture of mental processes which in every other area of thought tend to be mutually exclusive. To the extent that contemporary prose fiction is unique, and even admirable, it tends to incorporate the cognitive density of criticism with poetry's traditional technical effects.

As our apprehension of the world becomes increasingly fictional, as fiction becomes an adjunct of all other disciplines, that which advertised as "actually" fictional becomes increasingly arbitrary. Once we begin to think about our fictions *within* them, fiction begins to lose the distinctiveness which always set it apart from poetry and criticism, which is to say, its aura of *commerce,* its historical role in the formation of mass culture. To the precise degree that it ironizes and interiorizes narrative, fiction eschews its mass audience. But at the same moment fiction dispenses with 19th century aesthetics, it can never quite give up gracefully, as poetry and criticism have, the 19th century sense of audience as *customer;* that somewhat sordid but finally unshakable link with reality.

18. The Critic as Artist

*Boundless the Deep, because
I am who fills Infinitude, nor
vacuous the space.*

—Paradise Lost

Contemporary fiction has been variously described as self-reflexive, involuted, solipsistic, cerebral, hermetic, privatized and cut off from the sources of life — yet is it not odd that we find these qualities even more profoundly illustrated in recent critical discourse? In 1924, I. A. Richards could write that "critics have as yet hardly begun to ask themselves what they are doing or under what conditions they work"; they can hardly be accused of ignoring such questions recently. Contemporary criticism has chosen to adopt the novelistic assumptions of the inseparability of form and content, the strategies of the self-referential voice, in order to erect a framework and radical rhetoric to legitimize the sources of its own waning authority. While the contemporary novelist is certainly bewildered about his lay audience, the critic is far more affected in his role by the destructive effects of the media. The artist's relationship to audience has always been historically problematic, indeed the subject of much of his work; but the "man of letters" has always been professionally defined by a literate lay audience, for which he in truth exists. He cannot court indifference without the severest consequences. The one absolutely intelligible event of Post-Modernism is the eradication of the Man of Letters by the professional academic.

The inability of the critic to find a usable language — beyond those codes which pass for professional accreditation — does not express mere contempt or elitism. What it reflects is that the critical function is becoming socially useless — we are seeing nothing less than the relinquishment of the facilitative intelligence, of the *mediative* role. We have come a long way from the Leavisite "tyranny of standards," to what might be called a "tyranny of methods."

Robert Scholes has written with feeling about this:

> Once we knew that fiction was about life and criticism was about fiction — and everything was simple. Now we know that fiction is about other fiction, is criticism in fact, or metafiction. And we know that criticism is about the impossibility of anything being about life, really, or even about fiction, or finally, about anything. Criticism has taken away the very idea of 'aboutness' from us. It has taught us that language is tautological, if it is not nonsense, and to the extent that it is about anything, it is about itself. Mathematics is about mathematics, poetry is about poetry, and criticism is about the impossibility of its own existence. ["The Fictional Criticism of the Future"]

If fiction has somewhat clumsily but persistently moved to appropriate its own critical space, nothing could be more revealing of the critical faculty than that it advertises itself as seamless, arbitrary and indeed as mysterious as the works of art it proposes to examine. This assertiveness reminds us that, true to its etymology, the essay is in fact the *freest* and most personal of all literary forms; no fiction can have the localized power or the allusiveness of critical discourse, for the simple reason that criticism can incorporate any mind, idea or voice without converting it to a credible *dramatis personae*. Yet never before has criticism been so hermetic and highly personalized. At the same time that artists subject art to critical strategies, criticism incorporates the prerogatives of artistic self-glorification and megalomania. At the very moment the artist has lost his traditional prestige and privilege, the critic arrogates them to himself. If innovations in criticism have taught us anything over the last two decades, it's that the deepest tautology still leaves something to be desired, that irony alone, no matter how sophisticated, can only take you so far, and that nothing is quite so tired as a tired novelty.

To put it another way, there is something about the relentlessness of radical epistemological doubt in so much contemporary criticism which suggests not a deliberate restructuring, but a rehash of the conventions of cultural relativism and linguistic determinism long ago exhausted by avant-garde literature, a criticism circumscribed not by

its own ingenious tautologies, but by its very banality. Consider Harold
Bloom: "Criticism is the discourse of the deep tautology — of the
solipsist who knows that what he means is right, yet that what he says
is wrong." This is not just a tautology. It is yet another variant on the
theme, "I know what I like." One recalls Pound's immortal judgment
of *Finnegans Wake.* "Only a divine vision or cure for the clapp could
justify this circumnambient peripherization."

Where critics find manic disorder, zaniness for its own sake, or
playing games by one's own rules as characteristic of recent fiction,
and then go on to imply that criticism is an analogous enterprise, then
criticism must be accountable to the charges normally brought to bear
upon art; i.e., clarity, symmetry, interest, the merit of ideas expressed
and the qualities of feeling produced. If criticism *is* fiction, let us then
prefer and honor any Barthelme story where such a voice would have
the parodic status it deserves.

It is a fascinating thing to consider that we are dealing here with
incommensurable monologues which cannot be tested by experience,
but only by another text. If we cannot return to the provincial idea
that criticism ought to serve the life and literature of its own time,
certainly we can argue with a criticism which so programmatically insists
upon its autonomous hegemony, whose structures correspond less to
the world than the most surrealist art. This is not to denigrate the critical
act as secondary, as Barth and Bellow do. Indeed we have many
examples of criticism rising above the art it proposes to examine. Roland
Barthes's argument for the "new novel" is more exciting and incisive
than any of Robbe-Grillet's attempts at it.

But we must nevertheless ask some simple-minded questions. Is there
not some difference between a "fine book" and a "text among others"
and is not that a legitimate question for criticism? What is our proper
reaction to be when in the name of "demystification" a text becomes
totally obscured by its interpretation? When Bloom says that "the
meaning of a poem can only be another poem," *[The Anxiety of
Influence]* would he apply that principle to his own essay? And if "all
literary criticism is prose poetry" and "prose poetry is verse criticism,"
how are prose and poetry to be distinguished from literary criticism?
This is neither deep nor tautological; it is simply unclear. Criticism *is*
artistic in that it ought to intensify and clarify perception —not make
it impossible.

What has happened is that the aggressive bluff and bravado associated historically with Avant-Garde attitudinizing, which so many contemporary writers are at pains to avoid, is now a stance available to the critic — the critic as cultural desperado. It brings to mind Stendhal's definition of a decadent: "one who sacrifices himself to passions which he does not possess."

From a social viewpoint, it is clear that a criticism which is "pure," unreferenced, and above all *unprecedented* is dictated by the need to open up new means of professional accreditation and advancement, and that it betrays the same unconscious fear experienced by the artist — that one is free precisely because no one cares.

The attempt to assert literary criticism as *the* presiding and autonomous discipline, to usurp the prerogatives of both art and philosophy, only accentuates the fact that the culture now operates well beyond any literary frame of reference. Lest the "creative" writer dismiss these critical impulses as Mandarin delusion, he should be reminded that they are precisely the same psycho-cultural characteristics that are to be found in current fiction — the same fear of isolation masked by an insistence upon autonomy, the same nagging notion that everything has been done, the same hatred of the journalistic and rejection of humanistic values, the same absolutist aggressivity of the reader turned writer with a vengeance, and the same self-indulgence evident when the normal constraints of justifying one's work to *any* audience are removed.

If the artist in these circumstances takes refuge in aestheticism, the critic retreats to philosophy, thinking he may free himself of the "bewitchment of intelligence by the means of language." It should not be surprising that this enterprise should prove so circumlocutory. As Leszek Kolakowski has pointed out, "Even if the society of knowledge should succeed in showing how the complete freedom of the knowing mind from the impact of particular group interests is possible, and what freedom should mean, *it would leave the epistemological question precisely where it was*. A hypothetical 'purified' mind could go on indefinitely asking itself the question whether, now that it is free of the distortions incurred by the social milieu, it lives in conditions of 'essential rationality' — and it would be powerless to resolve this question."

But there is also a more serious or at least a more dramatic question here. Far from providing an equilibrium of objective relations, the contemporary critical impulse pushes one beyond a consideration of transmitting culture, to breaking it up and making it over in one's own image — hence the semi-hysterical attempts to erase whatever distinctions remain between criticism and literature.

While fascinating in itself, criticism simply does not create the aesthetic consciousness which it proposes to examine. Yet when criticism does penetrate *just far enough* into non-discursive experience, there is often the realization that there *are* language acts which place the critic's honest worry, restraint and scrupulousness in a severely reduced perspective. It remains an unquestionable and sobering historical fact that no significant fiction writer of recent memory has turned to any theorist for any kind of reciprocal relationship, and no theorist of any real force has taken the writing of his contemporary fiction writers as a departure point for his own work. So much for autonomy.

We have educated ourselves thoroughly in the psychopathology of contemporary art, but we will not understand our time until a mind appears which can demonstrate the phenomenon of the critical mind turning upon itself, frequently producing a truly hallucinatory quality, freakish posturings directly at odds with the very processes (if we can no longer speak of values) it sees itself as promoting. The ideal reader has become, like the ideal artist before him, a kind of monster. No other intellectual discipline would be permitted to deploy its own vulnerability in such a strategic fashion. Nor would such outrageous *talk* be countenanced from anyone with less obvious self-hatred. Yet in its bizarre displacement of intellectual energy, its linguistic delirium, criticism remains a cracked mirror of the culture.

19. The Poet as Person

Wherever I am, I am what is missing.

—*Mark Strand*

If through the mutual expropriation of each other's territory, fiction and criticism have expanded their available repertoires, contemporary poetry has, by disacquainting itself with all its progenitive forms save the low short lyric, ceased to struggle for its own aesthetic.

If fiction and criticism have, often with a spectacular lack of success, attempted to have repercussions beyond their own traditional linguistic areas, poetry has managed a startling retrogression to the *prosaic*.

And if fiction and criticism can be legitimately disparaged for veering towards the abstract and even unreadable, poetry has seemed content to settle for idle conversation.

Against the strident willfulness of contemporary prose, poetry effects an atmospheric aimlessness. The archetypical Post-Modern poem may sound like myth, and look like a dream, but adds up to an enumeration of non-propositions, giving a new meaning to the word "automatic," which began in the glory of unconscious association and has ended up as mere preprocessed designation.

In poetry's technically diffuse and intellectually insipid diction, a failed Transcendence constitutes a deliberate code in which the most conventional statements are given portent by simply dissolving their most obvious narrative rendering. If fiction has had to contend with a caricatural twin based on popular clichés, poetry has constructed formulae almost entirely upon intellectual clichés — an aesthetic mode acceptable by the conspicuousness of its anti-conventions. Neither lyric nor narrative, poetry has come to insist upon its *occasional* quality as an aspect of literature commissioned expressly for the margin.

"Free verse has been the great equalizer," Mary Kinzie notes, "liberating poetic speech to utter the small impression in homely language, but at the same time creating its own built-in obstacle to the registering of the leisurely and complex idea. . . ." And what Mark Van Doren remarked twenty years ago seems all the more applicable now.

> The possible importance of poetry is immense at any time. And why not now? I would make no exception of our time though there are those who do. They are the ones who persist in identifying poetry with short poems, and who even then do not remember how great a short poem can be — for it can be dramatic, too, and somehow narrative; it can imply careers, for ideas and for men. The short poem is better in those ages when the long poem is better; or, at the minimum, when it exists. The forms of literature reinforce one another, as tragedy and comedy do, which are the forms of thought. When fiction is good, then poetry can be good; and vice versa. Fiction indeed *is* poetry; or as I have put it here, poetry is story. This is not my idea, as you very well know; it is at least as old as Aristotle, and it has prevailed whenever poetry has been important to people. . . . But when I say fiction do I mean merely narratives or dramas in verse? Not necessarily. The ancient categories of lyric, epic, and dramatic poetry were not conceived in terms of verse alone, and it is fatal for us to suppose so. What we call prose fiction today is in fact the most interesting poetry we have. *[The Happy Critic]*

Once defining itself by rarity and purity, poetry has become the most democratic of literary art forms, an antidote, it is true, to the social resignation reflected in fiction and criticism. As such, with the possible exception of science fiction, poetry claims the only coherent audience in literary culture, an audience held together by the appropriation of non-verse as a performing art, a medium which belongs to the group. When you have embraced *minima*, when closure is the only definitive effect, when the reader must draw all implicit conclusions for himself, when metaphor is not elaborated but only signified by a dropped definite article, and when marginal space becomes the major organizing principle, then one is left with an appeal to the pretextual communication of a "reading," the dramaturgy of a "personality" in a tribal situation. This is hardly a resuscitation of a participatory, mnemonic "oral tradition" but the monotonous grammar of a precocious child; the recitation of a written text which attempts to reestablish a rapport with the audience through pseudo-kinetic kinship. This fashion of homeless orality is only the final instance of nostalgia for populist primitivism taken up by academic terrorists in its most cerebrized form. "The writers of today feel this," Roland Barthes tells us; "for them, the search for a non-style or an oral style, for a zero level or a spoken level of writing is, all things considered, the anticipation of a homogeneous social state . . . [!]"

Whereas fiction has exploded its personae and criticism has deregulated itself, poetry has found itself disappearing into the page in its quest for the essential, and rather than accepting the fate of this project of exhaustion, it has translated itself into a minor media event which provides, if not community, at least a kind of corporate engagement: immediacy as false intimacy in a grotesquely artificial extended family.

Post-Modern poetry is neither concrete nor mystical, but has become the least allusive and most predictable form of contemporary literature; a true shorthand based not upon compression but the contemporary preference for abbreviation — a scenario for untransmitted feelings, exemplifying above all a time which exceeds the artist's understanding.

It remains the vanguard of the arts only in the sense that disintegration shows up there first.

20. Banal Antagonists: From Campus to Television

The bourgeois production and publication apparatus can assimilate, even propagate, an astonishing mass of revolutionary themes without putting its own existence into serious doubt. . . . The instant the criterion of authenticity ceases to be applicable to artistic production, the total function of art is reversed.

—*Walter Benjamin*

It was not so long ago that Malraux remarked that American literature was the only literature not written by intellectuals, echoing the stupefying preference of the French for our most brainless writers, from Poe to Hammet. To say that Post-Modernism is an intellectual's art is dubious, for it is no longer possible to distinguish between intellectuals and those who are just going through the motions in this strangest, most recent and rapidly growing class. What is clear is that the Post-Moderns are the first generation of American writers with the common denominator of a college education, which only means they came of age as Art was becoming simply another province of opinion in the intellectualization of modern life. They overlap an era which carried Modernism's program of retraining all of the senses to a bureaucratic conclusion, finally rendering the idea of *any* curriculum as suspect. Rich in procedures, it is a generation which lacks a subject matter.

Perhaps it is more specific to say that there are fewer writers than ever before who can claim to be ignorant of literary history. Most have been exposed to the idea of writing as intellectual vocation as well as romantic inclination, and they take ideas and procedures as seriously as emotions. ("Don't think," Fitzgerald warned his contemporaries. "Anybody can think.") At the same time, there seems to be an almost total estrangement between practitioners and theorists, complicated perhaps by their superficial proximity within the Academy, and the fact that they echo one another's concerns without acknowledging each other.

The serious charge which Bellow favors is that the inclusion of writers into universities for the last thirty years has cut them off from "real life"; indeed that Post-Modernism is merely indicative and most foully derivative of the academization of culture, a critique which certainly has some merit. Nevertheless, it should be clear by now that working for Hollywood, or the WPA, or exile to the cafe society of a foreign culture is no less destructive than wasting away in a university; it is also apparent that there is no more cross-fertilization among writers and literary academicians than between writers and astrophysicists. Perhaps this is inevitable, as what is fobbed off as self-evident to the practitioner always remains (and properly so) an open question to the theorist. The codification process by which academics once excluded "living authors" now absorbs them, as the expanding research market and the demand for "creative" or contemporary courses require. Who wants to annotate the uncollected reviews of Yeats when one can "mark a water shed in the history of modern sensibility as an imaginative political and ultimately spiritual reality . . . the history not only of writing, but of the indispensable subtext and pretext of writing, the way we live our lives and attempt to make sense of those lives . . .[!]" (Frank McConnell)

At any rate, given the heterogeneity of current writing, it would be pretty difficult to deduce a "school" of influence from an employment situation. We know that patronage like parentage exacts its dependencies, and that no satisfactory patronage system has ever been devised. But when looking for literary cause and effect it is often fruitful to ask a simple social question. Our culture has chosen to subsidize writers by employing them to teach the young, hardly an ignoble or antihumanistic impulse. And the proper question is not whether this has affected writers, but whether this is the best way to make use of writers. How does their academic involvement relate, for example, to the historically unprecedented decline in general literary and educational proficiency? The fact remains that writers have been included in faculties only since general education standards were chucked. The issue is not whether writers have been somehow circumscribed, but whether society can afford to have its most literate (if hardly its most wise) in the service of protracted adolescence? Conversely, writers might ask themselves why the American writer is the furthest removed from the productive relations of his society, further removed than his literary counterpart in any other western culture, including totalitarian ones.

Just as publishing companies merged to effect increasing economies of scale, contemporary literature was merged into the university because of its relative market share in the loss-leading industry of the Humanities. As a commodity in a mixed economy, it was acquired not as an asset, but as a product line, designed to enhance a curriculum which had reflected, more than anything, absolute indifference to an extra-professional market. It now constitutes a new service industry in an enterprise benumbed by a quarter century of reckless growth. If commercial fiction is marketed increasingly as Opinion, in the university it became marketed precisely as Technique. Needless to say, it could only happen in America.

The transition from Literary Modernism to Post-Modernism is accomplished by the determination to spread elitist art through populist assumptions and intensive capitalist methods. It is no wonder that the Post-Modern writer cannot understand himself as the product of an ameliorative evolution.

The university is like any other corporate entity; it can ignore, censor, or facilitate artistic enterprise. It can certainly neither create nor defeat it. The only charge that can be fairly brought against the modern university is also the severest — a genuine lack of curiosity and purpose as regards the reintegration of knowledge, and a professional structure which makes any intellectual reform impossible. It will remain notable primarily for producing the first generation in American history less skilled than their parents.

*   *   *

The opening of genre, which is literary Modernism's most enduring legacy to the contemporary, becomes accelerated as literary conventions are absorbed into those of mass communications. What begins as a self-willed rearrangement of intellectual property comes full circle in the electronic media, in which the producers of art are totally dispossessed. With television, both history and fiction as aesthetic categories become increasingly meaningless, as their traditionally uneasy relations and irregular contours are flattened out. It is precisely the byplay between the temporal and the historical which provides fiction with its peculiar perspective, a cross-processing which its consumer must also undergo, and which television delimits by its very nature. Post-Modern fiction emphasizes the flux of various overlapping realities in order to intensify the process of selective association. If fiction stresses signification as it proceeds, television is the medium which is least possible to think about as it is occurring. It dis-integrates by signifying everything in advance. If fiction is characterized by inner proliferation and compound instability, television claims a perfect unity of form and homogeneity of content. When we complain about television's "superficiality," what we are really saying is that its very process *deliberately empties reconstituted experience of its literary content* — not necessarily, we should add, a bad idea. Nevertheless, television reconstitutes the very narrative conventions of anticipatory truth which every major writer since Flaubert has ironized. What distinguishes a "made for television" production is that it adopts the 19th century narrative conventions bypassed by the pure cinema, which tends to exploit the techniques anticipated by literary Modernism. It picks up with a vengeance the inflationary tradition of the romance, a Romanesque world of idealized types, the basic formulae of Literal Revivalism. It is almost as if television were invented to smooth out the cognitive dissonances which Modernism celebrated.

It is the adaptation, the *scenario*, which has become the primary literary convention of the age, one that invades all disciplines, from cybernetics to psychoanalysis. This will be our legacy, this filmic shorthand where narrative is moved appropriately to the margin as lighting instructions; description is reduced to a single bracketed adjective, characterization to role, the common vernacular to a series of ellipses, and dialogue to its most attenuated and formulaic — an abbreviated reality shaped above all by a concept of time which is money, adapting symbolic (literary) language to machine (market) language.

This development should not be reduced to a question of "high" versus "low" art. With the scenario and the adaptation, we are simply dealing with a willfully inferior form of cognition.

The Electronic media fear nothing so much as the historical sense: its contemplativeness, its revisionism, its circumlocution, the inevitable corrections and abrasions of contrasting perspective. Commodity values are threatened by the historical reflection which has always represented the beginning of fiction's territory — memory resuscitated by the imagination. This is hardly news and we must be quite precise about the effects of the institution of television, which is capable of destroying any other institution in the culture. For the perniciousness of television is not that it serves up vulgar entertainment, that as sensory deprivation it functions as a mass sedative, that it incites violence in children, or even that it fires 25,000 volts of phosphorescent light per second into our endocrine systems; it is that it treats all events as a *story*. TV is *total* Aristotle, and it is *story at all costs*, not realism *per se*, which becomes the characteristic expression of contemporary bourgeois society.

This idiotic and endless storification of experience ignores not only the complexity of language but the plasticity of life. The chief complaint of a trial football game without "commentary" (December 20, 1980) was that the viewer lacking commentary *"needed too much concentration to enjoy the game*. Even then he or she received too little story line . . . " If Post-Modern fiction can be characterized by any single movement, it is precisely the momentum away from the exaggeration of dramatic conflict, skeletal events as history, the focus upon a single stimulus or metaphor as the index to reality; away from the easily purchased analogies which storification affords.

The appropriation of the most superficial of narrative conventions by the media means that the Post-Modernist affection for the counter-genre will only intensify. Already at several removes, the autonomous writer will continue to take as his point of departure the shattering of the official narrative line. To be "literary" in such a context is to choose disassociation and disaffection as the primary values. "There was a rankling indignity," Scott Fitzgerald writes in *The Crack-Up*, "that to me had become almost an obsession, in seeing the power of the written word subordinated to another power, a more glittering, grosser power . . . whether in the hands of Hollywood merchants or Russian idealists [it] was capable of reflecting only the tritest thought, the most obvious emotion." It is obvious that a sense of indignity is not sufficient to sustain any integrated literary career.

If concept can transform reality, so can lack of concept, absence of *any* perspective. If Modernism insisted that cognition can grow independently, television has demonstrated that it can also decrease collectively. When Walter Benjamin said that storytelling in the 20th century was moribund, in an age in which man is "increasingly unable to assimilate the data of the world around him by way of experience," he could not envision the replicatory power of Television. It is one of the supreme ironies of contemporary life that literature, so aestheticized by Modernism, mocked by Joyce as 'ABCDE-Mindedness,' should have been moved closer to "experience" by a pictographic medium which neither requires nor develops any skills associated with adulthood. In such a context it is not surprising that fiction should no longer oppose itself to non-fiction, or to a theory of unitary realism, but to the conventions of storytelling formalized by the mass media.

Insofar as literature ever provided a social frame of reference, it has been obliterated by the two growth industries of the Post-Modern era — the democratized academy and the mass entertainment industry. The academy absorbs literature as a subsidiary, a paper acquisition in which assets are not redeployed but only displayed more attractively on a newly consolidated balance sheet. It is formally but not functionally integrated into the curriculum, an idealized form devoid of content.

The media, on the other hand, through the obsessive use of the very narrative conventions Modernism discredited, endlessly recirculates content, to produce an aura which makes the spectator experience an equally non-existent reality, employing all the conventions of Realism in the distortion of real life.

Both of these pseudo-integrations, oligopolistic centralizations of technology and certification which pass themselves off as unified repositories of culture, relinquish the idea of an audience which is *alterable*, as both refuse to take responsibility for *what* is taught. Here is the final expression of an inflationary commodity culture which assigns to content only exchange- rather than use-value.

The situation no longer reflects the Modernist one-on-one confrontation between the reader and writer. Modernism still operates within the classical supply and demand dialectic of buyer and seller; the Post-Modern adds an incalculable third dimension to the equation in the predominance of the media and the academy as market-makers. The trajectory of intellectual "despair," which began when the historical optimism associated with the New Deal and the struggle against Nazism broke down, cannot be fully explained by the political disillusionment of the left, some existential malaise, or linguistic alienation. A more straightforward view is that despite the mythologies of autonomy, intellectuals cannot function without institutions of communication, and the fact remains that the two institutions which constitute the "consciousness industry" have become not only progressively sterile and debased, by any external standard, but have refused, almost as a matter of principle, to make their own worlds coherent. It goes without saying that there is very little in the Modernist tradition which prepares us to deal with either of these two "Post-Modern" establishments.

In the Post-Modern era, just as the consumer is bathed in information which has no principle of differentiation, so art is bathed in intellectual speculation — the result in both cases being the cynical bewilderment of a populace initially perplexed by jargon, then finally condemned to repeat it.

21. Of The Future [Sic]

> You see, literature is not so bad.
>
> —*Brooks and Warren*,
> Understanding Fiction

The legacy of interiority becomes for the writer an increasingly defensive antidote to the external media, while for the theorist it becomes a bastion to be defended from bourgeois homogeneity. This adds a new element to the writer's quandary, for on the one hand he is dismissed by the media (as insufficiently translatable), and on the other, by indeterminist critics, who deprive his arbitrary language of any evidential basis. He is caught ultimately between the market which fixes a formulaic meaning in advance, and a theory which, also in advance, denies his work any potential meaning. The greatest danger to the contemporary writer is not that he will "sell out" to the media, but that he will write merely against it — to destroy the clichés of storification by an uncritical obsession with the deflationary counter-genre.

Even if we began now to reverse the culture's indifference to thought processes associated with reading and writing, no one writing today would live to see the results. The trends, insofar as a minority literate culture are concerned, appear irreversible. The argument that the novel is itself a product of technological change, and that, given its head, technology will respond to minority culture, ignores the fact that it is not production but transmission costs which are finally decisive, and the fact that contemporary literature has only two arenas — the tax sheltered university or high-roller show business. The audience for serious writing is, as the market jargon has it, a *mature* audience, one whose growth is severely limited, and whose interests are therefore negligible. Late capitalism and climax inflation cannot respond to mature markets. Inflation creates an economy in which there is no place to hide.

The final stage of Post-Modern inflation sees the reallocation of all cultural resources to the big ticket items, for no consensus exists as to which cultural activities have value. This tendency is given a final bizarre fillip with stagflation, when prices continue to rise while demand actually decreases. In such a situation, only the largest borrowers can continue to play the game immoderately, so that any response to short term opportunity can only be made at another's expense. Such is the disruptive anomie of drastically shortened horizons and unprecedented uncertainty, when capital cannot be allocated to any long term undertakings.

The cultural pluralism which was Modernism's special promise has been destroyed to the extent that technology is not responsive to a developed political and social will. Technology has replaced industrialism in modern pessimism as the metaphor for a failure of nerve.

It is easy in such frustrating circumstances to fall into technophobic cant. The liberal progressive ideal maintains after all that advances in technology will ultimately make available increased choice at a reduced cost to the consumer. But it is now clear that in an inflationary context, the audience is not so much specialized as fragmented, so that the costs of quality become overwhelming. Every advance in hardware results in a further standardization of software. Even the richest corporations cannot sustain the costs of reaching a minority audience, as the recent fiasco in cable TV demonstrates. Rather than a cornucopia of specialized services, we have an increasingly limited number of alternatives, all aimed at a mass audience. For what happens in American-style inflation is that, lacking social coherence or political leadership, the management of mass psychology is turned over to the Media and Academy. These institutions are capable of absorbing hostilities and resentments by appearing to appeal to all competing groups simultaneously, but to accuse them of censorship or repression is to miss the point, for neither institution has a coherent social or political viewpoint other than to respond in terms of their "measurable" audience responses. Thus the Academy dilates content as the media dilutes it, putting into question any inherent value in "education" or "entertainment," a process in which the only common denominator is a vague collective helplessness.

Such a system does not require totalitarian political or social control mechanisms because the system adjusts its feedback to match our output — which is why its prophecies tend to be self-fulfilling and criticism of it, circular. As opposed to classically authoritarian forms of control, it appears benign, because it operates without any cultural pride and feeds on its absence. The result is the absorption of art by the intelligentsia and the loss of control by the Bourgeoisie over its own culture.

If the academy has made the "experience" of literature available to anyone regardless of talent or interest, television is the ultimate expression of a culture which intrinsically denies participation by cost of entry, masquerading as a democratic form because everyone can "experience" it. In both cases, the mode of transmission, the market-maker, becomes the dominant reality. The culture becomes defined solely by markets for culture. For "markets" are certainly easier to find than audiences. Or, to put it another way, the problem with our pluralistic culture is that it is not very pluralistic — if by pluralism we mean an appropriate response to different kinds of art in a manner appropriate to each. It is the basic contradiction of Post-Modernism that its well-advertised pluralism of mind is not reflected in its agencies of cultural transmission.

As inflation hyperpluralizes the social and political order, it progressively negates cultural pluralism. And it is one of the preeminent lessons of the post-war period that cultural control does not require a political hegemony.

V.

22. Fiction as Forgetting

> . . . The Demand of that Species of Writing is over, or nearly
> so. Other Booksellers have declared The same thing. There was
> a Time, when every Man of that Trade published a Novel, 'till
> The Public became tired of them.
>
> —A Bookseller to Samuel Richardson, 1759

If we are to take much recent literary criticism seriously, the novel
appears to be the most short-lived, abortive art form in the history of
narrative literature: historically, only a holding action of the bourgeois
mind between the demise of epic poetry and the rise of modern cinema;
methodologically, simply a convenient device for those social scientists
of the last century, who, lacking statistical technique and electronic
communication, had to content themselves with what Goethe called
"mere narrative." And *mere* is still the adjective most appropriate to
the novel's condition.

It was some fifty years ago, in Madrid [within the year that *The Great
Gatsby, In Our Time, An American Tragedy, The Magic Mountain,
The Counterfeiters* and *Passage to India* were published elsewhere] that
we were first told with any assurance that the novel was dying. For
José Ortega y Gasset, the genre seemed no longer "an exploitable
mine," but rather "a stock of objective possibilities" which were being
exhausted. As is so often the case, the critic's own terminology furthered
the very dehumanization of art he described. To see the novel as a non-
renewable resource is, in itself, the basis for discovery that it is running
down. The aporia has become just as deterministic as any unitary theory
of art.

Nevertheless, Ortega was prescient in locating the crisis of the modern
novel in the question of admissable content itself. If the artist must

"care about his imaginary world more than any possible world . . . where shall we find new material to reconstruct the world?" In retrospect, it is not so important that we became incapable of believing in the Epic hero and his ranted recitations; but if we could no longer believe in *Him*, how could we possibly believe in *any* omniscient narrator? It is at such a point that art could no longer claim the sanction of religion, magic, even history; in other words, it could not be trusted simply because it appeared within a recognizable "frame" or was related by some putatively "authoritative" voice from the third balcony.

The very idea of the novel often elicits a response of desperation. Do we *believe* in the characters? Do we *trust* the narrator? What do these questions have to do with art? Do we ask whether we *trust* a composer, a painter? Do we *believe* in Marvell's coy mistress? No other art form elicits reactions which are ordinarily applied to human relationships. Yet this is the ultimate source of fiction's power: that it relies, often in spite of itself, upon powers not strictly linguistic — "the *mere* force," in Walter Scott's words, "of the excited imagination without material objects." Fiction is both theological and psychoanalytic at the same moment, in that it invokes a series of ritualistic unities simultaneously within a process by which they can be broken down and reassembled. No other art form betrays such a procedural uneasiness about its aesthetic existence. Yet in its cross-processing of abstract speculation and common sense revisionism, the pressure of the human upon the cerebral, lies the reason why the novel has been the dominant form of narrative for two centuries.

Nevertheless, as might be expected of a genre intrinsically related to middle class liberalism, the novel has constantly struggled to retain an authority it never had, to lay nostalgic grounds to be believed in, not only to take its place in art, but to insinuate itself into discourse about society. The history of the 19th century novel might then be viewed as a series of masks or stratagems compensating for the genre's questionable lineage. In this context, the romance emerges as the characteristic bourgeois response to the loss of omniscience — for the narrator, in directing himself to the idealizing tendencies of his audience, as well as to an attention span (genre) of *its* convenience, provides the illusion of authority regained. The reader becomes, in Ortega's words, a "temporal provincial"; the narrator's defects are disguised insofar as the reader adopts them for himself.

Naturalism, while its pretensions are anti-romantic, asserts its own authority just as surely to justify its scientific ways to man. "Is it not time to make justice a part of art," Flaubert asks, "so that art may attain the majesty of the law, the precision of science?" And within his work, the romance and the naturalism are enjoined through the autonomy of technique. No wonder we look back upon his century as the apogée of the genre. An audience can ask nothing more of an art form if it is both romantic in its procedure and scientific in its findings.

It was Joyce who broke up that happy marriage of convenience between the romance and naturalism by destroying the illusion of God speaking to the villager. And while Joyce may have believed with Flaubert that the personality of the artist finally refines itself out of existence, the effect of his having his narrator's mind working in full view of the audience is to insist upon the accountability of the narrator himself — beyond any frame or methodology — and to signal the reign of the "intellectual" in the arts.

Joyce did not exhaust the novel. He "merely" exhausted Omniscience as a point of view. The narrator could never again claim his form *ex hypothesi* in terms of audience needs or scientific method. Nor could the Bourgeois reader ever again dignify the romance as scientific. Next to Bloom, the epic hero is epicene. Next to Joyce, God comes off as simply a poor linguist and a monologist at that. And certainly the reader can no longer make it as a "temporal provincial."

There is some justification in treating the novel as dated, since it is, in fact, the oldest of abstract art forms, the first mixed-media. Its thrust from the beginning has been aleatory — syncretic, not synthetic — held together by the tension of its own formal contradictions, testimony both to the interpenetrability of experience and the necessity for recombinant expression. The novel has always exemplified an uneasy cohabitation between the empirical and the fictional impulses, which Ortega defined as the conflict between "scientific psychology" and "imaginary psychology."* The empirical grants the appearance of actuality, while the fictional indulges in the appearance of ideal system.

There are authors, in retrospect, for whom the conflict seems less overt: Flaubert, because he worked in a time when the romance was still venerable and science not yet suspect, and Joyce because he worked in a time when the destruction of every literary convention was still

---

*The terminology is as endless as it is clumsy. The Positivist draws the distinction between "verifiable" and "non-verifiable" experience, Proust between "involuntary" memory and "voluntary" memory, which is in service of the intellect. They are all Platonist throwbacks, and serve only to remind us, in Frank Kermode's words, that we always seem to prefer "an enigma to a muddle."

exciting, and not the working hypothesis of every freshman English class. In the present time, both candid conflict or potential reconciliation are often simply brushed aside and a certain exemplary tension is lost. There is no necessary clash between empirical and fictional for the epistemologist, because history for him is simply a way of looking at history, not an investigation of reality but of our experience of that reality. His narrator does not allude to events but describes the way we see events. As every man has become his own psychologist, every narrator has become his own epistemologist.

Be that as it may, the narrator who takes his perception absolutely for granted, as well as the narrator who trades obsessively on suspicion of his own perception, no longer seem authoritative as isolated voices. Both primitive realism and total subjectivism are impossible contemporary viewpoints, which is only to say that the updated ideological versions of both Literal Revivalism and Formalism are also open to serious question. A pure narration in which everything is imagined, or a strict presentation implying an exact mimeticism, simply cannot be pursued autonomously.

For after all, just as one cannot read history straight without trying to take into account one's own perceptual bias, neither can one gain access to history without at some point suspending the suspicion of one's perception. As Ortega says, "fiction is the act of forgetting," by which he means that one cannot make a fiction by simply hypothesizing or denouncing some projected equilibrium.

This is the most difficult thing for a critic to appreciate, not only because it is a process which cannot be described, but because it implies an intellectual *relinquishment*. As E.M. Cioran reminds us,

> To produce, to create . . . is to have the courage or luck not to perceive the lie of diversity, the deceptive character of the multiple . . . to produce a work is to espouse all those incompatibilities, all those fictive oppositions so dear to restless minds. More than anyone the writer knows what he owes to those semblances, these deceptions, and should be aware of becoming indifferent to them. If he neglects or denounces them, he cuts the ground from under his own feet . . . if he turns to the absolute, what he finds there will be, at best, a delectation in stupor . . . Anyone who is carried away by his reasoning *forgets* that he is using reason, and this forgetting is the condition of all creative thought. *[The Fall Into Time]*

But what if one rejects both the presumptions of the novel as history and history as epistemology? The arch reply to that question produced the most distinctive approach to fiction of the Post-Modern era, what journalists have come to call "black humor" and academicians, "dark comedy."

The essence of the method can be seen quite clearly in a slight book which purports to offer an analysis of the violence which underlies our society. And while it may be nothing else, James Purdy's *Cabot Wright Begins* is certainly a novel: a parody of the archetypal American W.A.S.P. within the archetypal American *picaresque*; refutation of both our conventional national experience and the traditional literary embodiment of it.

As in Nabokov, whom Purdy at his fleeting best most resembles, a false crisis in life is the metaphor for a genuine crisis in art. The plot does not suffer from encapsulization: novelist Bernie Gladhart is sent by his wife/muse Carrie Moore from Chicago to Brooklyn in search of the hero/rapist, Cabot Wright, lately released from prison, in order to "tell Cabot's story." Cabot is that "good subject" which Bernie hopes will give his otherwise undistinguished and overly personal prose some verisimilitude. Bernie discovers absolutely nothing, however; we find out about Cabot *in spite* of the storyteller, which certifies his modernity if nothing else. Actually, Cabot is located by one Zoe Bickle, wife of another failed novelist, Kurt Bickle; and Zoe, in collaboration with Princeton Keith, editor of editors, ghosts Cabot's story, though it is rejected in the end by Al Gugglehaupt, Goethe of publishers. Princeton is banished to his hometown in the midwest, Bernie is cuckolded in his absence by Joel Ullyae, super-swordman of color, and Zoe Bickle ends the book with perhaps the most anticipated climax in post-modern literature:

I won't be a writer in a place and time like the present.

Cabot's character development is worth pursuing since it obviously represents the novelist's answer to Ortega's concern with "caring about an imaginary world more than any other."

Cabot's fall from normalcy is traced to the fact that he was a "suppositious" or illegitimate child. But what plagues Cabot is not the fact of his background, but the jargon — psychological, journalistic, academic, and literary — which purports to explain him *in terms* of his background. The question is not so much one of Cabot's unsuitability as heir to the traditional American Dream, but his insufficiency as protagonist to the traditional omniscient narrator. The problem is that the "background" upon which Cabot's violence is based (and more importantly, the movement of the plot itself) is destroyed when we discover that he did not know about his questionable paternity until *after* he was released from prison — so that the cause for his rampage (more than 300 rapes in the Manhattan area alone) can hardly be attributed to that. Indeed, when finally cornered by Zoe Bickle, all Cabot can recall is that he started "feeling tired" one day, and that his wife and employer urged him to see a psychoanalyst, who promptly, after diagnosing his sickness as "chronic American Fatigue," suspended him from a padded meathook and liberated his libido. Thus unrepressed, Cabot "gets deadly" and attempts to satisfy his new found sexual strength, first through his wife who eventually can't keep up with him, and then upon the female population at large. While this is going on, his wife is committed to "the nut-hatch," his parents are killed in the "revolutionary Carribean," and these "tragic events" are once again enlisted by his village explainers as causal agents in his demise, except that again, Cabot discovers them *ex post facto*. It is clear that Purdy is trying to give the lie to any kind of conventional rationale — in terms of plot or psychology — that would claim to *explain* Cabot's behavior. As soon as any one narrator smacks of omniscience, he is struck down by conventional wisdom.

What is being rejected, however, is not only the scientific pretension to explain human behavior discursively, but also the literary presumption of Aristotelian complication and denouément. Purdy's vision consists of an autonomous, inexplicable action enveloped by a series of commentators who cumulatively pervert it. And the "tragedy" is that in the inexorable operation to define his "flaw," Cabot is gradually deprived of any identity whatsoever. His personality is overdigested until it becomes suitably surreal to others and unreal to him. Indeed, in the end, the only explanation he can offer is that he raped out of "boredom," which is, of course, both more plausible and dramatic than the other alternatives. As Cabot says:

> *I have lost my memory for consecutive events . . . I have read so many variations of what I did I forgot myself . . . I have heard my life so many times, I am a stranger to the story itself.*

And there we leave the Post-Modern storyteller.

Purdy is at pains to avoid the two staples of popular literature, psychological motivation and sexual description. He refuses to be that "good narrator" as Cabot refuses to be that "good subject." We are told nothing about his formative experience except in the clichés of the American Dream, nor are we told precisely *what* has made Cabot tired, just *how* the psychoanalyst liberates him, the manner in which he accomplishes his rapes, or even how they felt. All we know is that he accomplished them "easily and well."

Such absence of characteristic fictional ingredients might well be traced to the *nouvelle vague*. Purdy's rebellion, however, is directed not merely at a philosophy of form, but against the whole of recent American literary experience. Whereas his French counterpart is suspicious of language and its effect on modern experience, Purdy mistrusts modern life and its effect on language. What Purdy reflects above all is the paranoia we have developed about communication itself: the feeling that the extensions of media have overreached us, that "the medium is the message" means simply that the medium perverts, no matter what the message. And in this context, "form" can hardly be understood as a preconceived phenomenon, or even a writer's prerogative. It becomes rather a recognition of a medium, alienated first by those who sell it and then by those who buy it — intellectual and commercial agencies alike. Like Cabot's "suppositiousness," the entire question of form becomes *ex post facto*, germane to consumers and critics only. The artist is viscerally suspicious of any signification in advance, of *any* explanation acceptable to the marketplace.

In many respects, Purdy is the *last* novelist. He carries Gide's ideas of the "pure" novel — one which would leave the greatest amount possible to the reader's imagination — to its logical if absurd conclusion. He exemplifies Joyce's implicit assumption that originality in literature derives from waiving *all* literary conventions. He is Tolstoy's noble narrator who can "explain" nothing of what he has seen. He exemplifies the "new novelist's" concern with art not only as creation but as negative critique. And he is Ortega's ultimate novelist, for certainly he has forgotten enough, though the critic might well point out that the narrator simply didn't know enough to begin with — an essential Post-Modern apprehension.

The ambivalence of such a stance need not be elaborated. For Purdy is as close to Camp as a serious writer can get without being its apologist — Camp being defined as the parody of that which is no longer worth parodying. After all, to "rape out of boredom" is a perfect metaphor for the aesthetic which attempts to destroy the clichés of life by infibulating them with the clichés of art.

* * *

The continuous attempt to reconcile the empirical and fictional impulses within the novel ought not to be regarded as some external conflict between idealized forms of perception, but rather in terms of a pragmatic evolution of historical consciousness, in which subjective behavior is contextualized in accordance with whatever determinism is currently fashionable.

In short, the novel possesses no inherent equilibrium, or rather inherently disrupts the very equilibrium it seems to constitute. This is why criticism tends to treat all fiction as a mystery to be solved, and why negative critiques of any novel are almost always based upon underutilization of capacity.

Equilibrium in fiction is achieved only through the hindsight of canonization or the less hierarchic judgementalism of category. The New Critics, for example, could demonstrate equilibrium in any genre or period, because their analytic mode was grounded in an organic, integral world-view. As the Second Revolution progresses, however, the explicatory method is preserved without any unifying world-view and thus tends to produce endless demonstrations of dissolving equilibriums.

The Avant-Garde tends to make such dissolution into a credo, creating a consensual adversary style the toxicity of which is mitigated only by its vagueness, while the Literal Revivalist hypothesizes a restorative force to get things back into line, ignoring the fact that once an equilibrium is broken, it cannot be restored simply by the repetition of old habits and customs.

The Formalist posits an "inner" equilibrium within the work of art, just as the Realist posits an equilibrium based on reciprocity and objective truth; both, it would seem, are equally arbitrary and tenuous assertions.

Against the equilibriums once defined by genre, style and period, Modernism then becomes characterized by an equilibrium which fails to hold, a model which originally glories in distortion, but which eventually becomes only a routinized disturbance available to any middle-class terrorist, finally exemplifying the incapacity of the system to employ even its destructive techniques to full effectiveness.

The Post-Modern subjects this standardized disequilibrium to a novel embellishment, for in destroying any partial equilibrium *as it goes along*, it parodies both resolutions of order and destruction itself. This is reflected in an indisputable internal dynamism, as both the constraints and the variables of the model are opened to question; but more often than not, such creative disequilibrium itself becomes static, a doctrinal technique which anticipates its own lack of resolution. Whereas truth was once anticipated by genre, such works advertise in advance that there is no truth to get at. Loss is not an experience to be undergone, but a working hypothesis.

What happens all too often is that any instability in the work of art is justified by reference to the aimlessness of the general culture, a powerful reduction which every one of us has found useful from time to time. The Post-Modern Artist becomes a specialist in pseudomorphosis, as he refuses, as a matter of principle, the appearance of a new equilibrium. Such a stance obviously lacks the heroism of the Modernist model, because it appears merely as an involuntary hedge against the volatility of the system.

This is not merely an aesthetically generated response. All of our experience tends to reinforce the notion that an equilibrium is destroyed and restored by external forces, and the entire thrust of Modernism presupposes a dynamic art mocking the static social order of Bourgeois stability. But what happens then to the novel, an art form with no inherent stability, when it encounters a culture which *itself* displays the inherent disequilibrium of inflation, a society in which it appears no stability is possible within existing institutions? In such a situation, the artist can no longer capitalize upon a temporary disequilibrium, because it is the norm; hence the redundancy of the Adversary style. In inflation *all* apparent gains are, more or less, due to disequilibrium. Both character *and* milieux are equally fluid. Operating in such an environment the artist, no less than the citizen, gives up trying to optimize his position, and all formulations, whether couched in revolutionary or conservative rhetoric, become subject to diminishing marginal control: i.e., each time a new method of control is used, it has diminishing effectiveness the next time. This produces a chronic malaise of which literary pessimism is only a minor aspect. In both art and society, inflation insures that defensiveness becomes the dominant practical and psychological orientation to the world.

The only antidote to such defensiveness is not to justify art's inexactitudes by the culture's confusion, but to reassert the fact that precisely because of its mixed character, fiction remains an unequaled medium for fusing the imaginative and analytical faculties. Purdy reminds us that though fiction may not be the highest use of the mind, it is a necessary response to the enfeeblement of those disciplines which claim legitimacy by association with a formalized and one-dimensional method of inquiry. Literary fiction's uniqueness is that it remains ineffably amateur, opposed to the guildsman's mentality which permeates the popular genre, as well as the professional methodologies of literary criticism, insofar as it unsystematically and unskeptically makes use of the entire range of human cognitive development — from the crudest personal experience to the most abstract speculation. It trades pragmatically with all institutionalized modes of thinking and deinstitutionalizes them undidactically. It violates every principle by which responsible interpreters try to legitimize a subject matter by limiting its scope and thus make it epistemologically responsible. The novelist remains, in Montaigne's words, "an investigator without knowledge, a magistrate without jurisdiction." Fiction's uniqueness, its rare and occasional superiority as a cognitive mode, as well as its unprecedented failure rate, is due to the fact that it cannot limit itself in advance, that it remains an artform without an ontology, much less any theory of continuity. This sloppiness, which misleads the naive into believing that all consciousness is potentially aesthetic, is only redeemed by the terrible arbitrariness of sustained effort, increasingly foreign to our age. Fiction remains the artform which requires the least apprenticeship, but the most endurance, both in its audience and its maker. And the novel's "form" remains the consequence, if not the resolution, of that impure struggle between our empirical guises and what's left of our consciousness. That this process of re-cognition should constitute its own subject matter, or that it turns out to be one drama that holds our attention in the long run, should not be surprising.

Insofar as the recombinant process of fiction presents a *problem*, it is only because the equilibrium it achieves has no meaning outside of the adjustment process which leads to it. The fictional process is finally impervious to decoding because the mind is incapable of enduring the tedium which would be necessary to retrace each teleological step of the process. In a dynamic framework, the equilibrium and adjustment

to the equilibrium must be analyzed simultaneously, and criticism
cannot finally accomplish this because it reflects the dichotomy between
its own heuristic description of literature, which is dynamic, and its
formal modeling, which is static.

The fictive nature of fiction is not the *scandal* so many theorists imply.
The problem is not inherent in language or genre, but in the crude
Platonist terminology which cannot describe or even isolate the circuitry
of cross-processing within the empirical/fictional model. If scientists
contented themselves with such a dogmatic description of neural stimuli
and response, we would still believe with the Greeks that the memory
was located in the pancreas. It is one of the strangest facts of modern
life that the complexity of mental processes which generally elicit
reverence and awe in the scientific observer (accounting perhaps in some
part for the high morale of the sciences) invariably produce only
lamentation in the literary mind. What the literary mind gone
philosophical often complains about is that the structures of the central
nervous system and the structures of language do not display a
mathematical relation; never mind that it could not comprehend it if
one did exist. "It is not urged against cuticles that they are not hearts,"
Santayana says, "yet some philosophers seem angry with images for
not being things, and with words for not being feelings . . ." What *is*
reasonably clear is that the language of the central nervous system is
structured differently from those languages to which our common
experience refers, that in fact every attempt of neurophysiology to locate
specific mental functions in a particular portion of the brain, tends to
reveal upon further investigation that the functions are *spread
throughout the system* — a mixed process, in other words, which resists
dialectical categorization. We still know next to nothing about these
components, and literary criticism is a singularly deficient discipline
for pursuing their interrelations, its "brain model" reaching a dead
end some time ago. If criticism has had to make an alliance with
linguistics, then it appears that linguistics will have to make further
alliance with neurobiology and biochemistry if it really is serious about
pursuing these questions. The "deep structures" of language do not
take us further into the text, but only further into the central nervous
system. There is very little left in literary criticism which would make
it more attractive than competing modes of scientific inquiry.

It is only with the development of "artificial" intelligence that we
have a set of metaphors which reaffirm the depth and complexity of

what Ortega called the "imagination." The one modern thing we know about the nervous system and its neuronal pools is that their interchange repeatedly changes character from digital to analog — a cross-processing between genetic determinism and learning, expressed both as a series of organizing techniques and as biochemical responses to actual conditions — or to put it in old-fashioned terms, a synchrony of the fictional and empirical impulses.* Dialectical antinomies are simply insufficient to explain the functioning of such a multiplexed network. In this regard, most literary criticism is on the level of an instruction book for operating a ten dollar single-reflex camera.

Fiction, then, might be understood as a set of individually unreliable elements which can nevertheless be designed to function with an arbitrarily high reliability, i.e., through its indisputably mixed character, "a deterioration in arithmetics has been traded in for an improvement in logics" [John Von Neuman, *The Computer and the Brain*] — yet another positivism amplified by a grudging accountability to unquantifiable human behavior.

When this habitual cross-processing is put in the context of comparative cultural history, fiction can be seen as neither transcendental project nor autonomous technique, but as the natural evolution of an intelligence which has had to deal with the antinomy between Realism — the imperviousness of things on the one hand — and the Formalist, idealistic tendency to locate everything in the mind. This most certainly does not mean that "everything is a fiction," or even that our apprehension of the world is primarily fictional — for that is to confuse fiction with mere storytelling and the increasingly empty and grandiose promises of art. It only serves to remind us that this antinomy represents an arrangement of knowledge not more than two hundred years old — that it is no accident that the concept of Modern Man parallels the development of the novel.

As fiction lacks an ontology, it has historically tended to advertise itself as something more procedurally deterministic than it is, "looking like" some kind of history or science in which every detailed occurrence can be correlated with its antecedents. Modernism, of course, is in

---

*"Human beings communicate both digitally and analogically. Digital language has a highly complex and powerful logical syntax but lacks adequate semantics in the field of relationship, while analogic language possesses the semantics but has no adequate syntax for the unambiguous definition of the nature of relationships." (Watzlawick, *The Pragmatics of Human Communications*)

essence a revolt against such simplistic cause and effect, and Post-Modernism, as we can see with Purdy, elevates the anomaly to the status of a law of Nature.

Moreover, literature can be read as a kind of barometer of the default of other disciplines; its strategy can often be best understood by considering what other more formalized discipline it is attacking, mimicking, or negotiating with. Even in its most defensive mode, for example, fiction expresses its sense of superiority to the Social Sciences, which tend to treat human experience in terms of grossly molar macroevents, whereas fiction tends to concentrate on the myriad microevents which even the most sophisticated theorist hardly ever perceives individually. With Purdy, we see the novelist's profound aversion to Psychology, that scientism most deeply embedded in mass consciousness, and it may well be this resolute if contemptuous indifference to simplistic psychological cause and effect which will be fiction's most enduring contribution to whatever revision of consciousness the contemporary eventually manages. It of course remains a surly fact of art that such anti-cause-and-effect often amounts to nothing more than a mere shrugging off of *any* pattern.

On the other hand, Post-Modern fiction's tendency to "look like" Philosophy, as it once looked like History, is a more questionable strategy. It is highly unlikely, because of its unsystematic character, that literature (or literary criticism) can ever provide starting points of inquiry, much less illuminate the generative base of its own procedures. As a matter of fact, it can be argued that fiction succeeds as a mediating experience only to the extent that it accepts its fate as an inherent disequilibrium, that it exercises its power in *escaping* its origins; in Merleau-Ponty's words, that "noble form of forgetfulness."

Fiction constitutes a jungle of ad hoc assumptions, abstract speculation and mere hunches, as well as mediation of direct experience. In this sense, the novel is a *barely* epistemological act, and at base is not even *literary*. The durability and uniqueness of fiction is above all due to the fact that the materialistic and the linguistic, the historical and the temporal, the real and the fabricated, tend not only to conflict, but also to perpetuate and reinforce one another. This making of a home for the temporality of all experience, for all anticoincidental mental processes, explains why almost everyone believes he has *this* particular art form, and only this one, the novel, within him.

23. The Use and Abuse of Death

"Do you know, Mr. Yule, that you have suggested a capital idea to me? If I were to take up your views, I think it isn't at all unlikely that I might make a good thing of writing against writing. It should be my literary specialty to rail against literature. The reading public should pay me for telling them that they oughtn't to read. I must think it over."

"Carlyle has anticipated you," threw in Alfred.

"Yes, but in an antiquated way. I would base my polemic on the newest philosophy."

—*George Gissing,* New Grub Street, *1891*

The most unpleasant aspect of contemporary alienation is that no one bothers to examine its aspects. As a metaphysical concept, it is diluted by high agnosticism; as a social concept, by the absorption of intellectuals into the middle class. It has now the currency of a major idea, which in our time means that it can be generally accepted without logical or personal consequences.

To dismiss apocalyptic criticism as a self-contained enterprise with little relation to the energies which actually produce and disseminate literature is fair enough; it is also easy enough to attribute the decreasing interest in serious literature to a conspiracy of greedy publishers and a distracted, mindless reading public. But those who have been preoccupied with literary culture during the age of the Death of Language, and with fiction during the Death of the Novel, owe such dismissals some specific scrutiny.

As any Trade Editor will confirm, serious fiction as a commercially viable item in the mass market is now undeniably moribund. To say, of course, that an art form which cannot pay its own way is also generically defunct is a respectable American argument; happily it is no longer applied to any other art form, from Grand Opera to aerial bombardment. It is somewhat closer to truth to say that it is almost impossible to raise money to capitalize or subsidize literature, the most obvious reason being that literature is both produced and consumed in private; thus it is difficult to involve patrons, by contrast with the performing arts, where an audience can, if not appreciate the production, at least achieve a collective sense of itself. What is worth pursuing is how the End-of-the-Genre Criticism dovetails so nicely and curiously with corporate apologetics about the lack of demand for fiction.

Let us pursue three assertions. (1) At the moment when America has an unusually diverse amount of compelling fiction, and (2) the novel and short story are undergoing significant innovation, (3) the response of the conventional market to fiction is as low as it ever has been. Now (1) cannot be proven — only exemplified — though it's available to any publisher who's willing to lose money. Item (2) remains in the domain of close textual analysis. But let us examine (3) in a rather simple-minded way — literature as a commodity. So we might regard writers, not as artists engaged in some vaguely transcendental project, but rather as artisans who have absolutely no control over the forces which produce and distribute what they make.

Literary Law #1: *Literature is the only art form in our generation whose technology and dissemination has not been radically challenged by its practitioners.*

Both the European tradition of art as a secular religion and the American predilection for artists as heroic or at least stoic *isolatos* have made it very difficult for American writers to question the mechanisms of publishing. It seems, if not hopeless, then beneath them, a vulgar materialism with which no serious artist should concern himself. This attitude denies community, we know; it also denies what even most established American writers have almost always done without: a sense of audience. I think it's fair to say that no serious fiction writer in America today can tell you whom he is writing *for*. We simply do not have the kind of reciprocity which Keynes spoke of when he said that H.G. Wells's mind "seemed to grow along with his readers." This is not death, but it is narcosis. It doesn't finally affect genius or human will, it can never be used as an excuse for failed experiments, but it does have serious cumulative effect on the development of fiction, as well as the health of a culture, as it forces us to rely on either a pride or a cynicism which is not earned.

Over the last two decades, our writers have become increasingly characterized by the extent of their brain damage; and fiction writing itself is continually described as a kind of timeworn self-indulgence in an increasingly nonverbal society, the last gasp of privatism and individualism in a world which can be saved only by destroying the last links to language, through some collective sensory experience beyond symbol and sign. We have rarely viewed our writers as functional craftsmen, and the refusal to accept artists as anything but madmen or eremites is not exactly new. But the fashion of celebrating writers for the damage they do themselves, seeing their power as commensurate with the pain they inflict, has reached a new intensity. The exemplary narrative voice of the era is paranoia, and self-loathing is the primary mode of our most popular poets. Our sense of self has been so diminished that fiction — whose traditional domain is the relation of the private self to its public contexts — was preempted by the confessional shriek, a cry so intense and deafening that it hardly requires narrative momentum. One feels a little nostalgic to recall that early in the sixties, we were told that what was "out there" was so fascinating that only documentary reportage could be equal to it, and this was cause enough for ignoring a fictional imagination which had somehow not kept pace with a magical reality. But in the end, that decade was chronicled in poetic fragments, in suicidal dreams, not by our *essayistes*.

If fiction could not keep pace with the "relevance" of the New Journalism, neither, it would seem, could it be adequate for a "counter culture" in which Reality became totally privatized. Its middle distance strategy was not serviceable for either the Think Piece or the Hallucination. And being told one is anachronistic is, after all, better than being told one is untalented or unpopular — it absolves everyone of responsibility. To be sure, such speculations do not confront the argument which proposes an intrinsic devolution of a genre. But that argument in turn fails to consider the extent to which we are determined not by *genre*, but by a hopelessly anachronistic technology and failed cultural agency. In other words, the cost of producing and marketing literature has simply exceeded its industry's profit margin, and this particular disease has been masked long enough by theories of dying forms and metaphors of terminal illness.

It doesn't take a Marxist to understand the effect of conglomerate mergers in trade publishing — it is the American fate of our time, and writers should not expect to be exempted from it more than anyone else.* But if we are absorbed by the deaths of certain traditions, we must understand that businesses, like genres, have their own cycles of expiration. In other words, conglomerates, given their internal capitalization needs, their salaries and wage structure, can compete only through constant expansion fueled by continuous breakthroughs in marketing and technology. This is not to suggest that conglomerate ownership automatically reduces the options of a publisher. Nonetheless, there seem to be some inexorable laws which affect what we call "serious" literature.

A conglomerate's products are measured by their "spin-off value." That is, products must replicate other products within interlocking systems. Hence the book, and the novel in particular, becomes defined by its *subsidiary* functions almost totally, movie and television rights being the typical example.

Lit Law #2: *The commercial life of a novel is exactly proportional to the extent to which it is translated into media other than its own.*

The flexibility as well as competitiveness of conglomerates was historically determined, in America particularly, by successive breakthroughs in technology. As artisans, we have a situation where there has been no advance in the science of making books since offset printing, and no advance in distribution whatsoever. As always, the weakness of the system is revealed most clearly in a hiatus of growth. The real costs of making this thing we call a book have more than

---

*The numbers are instructive. As of 1982, more than 50% of all mass market sales were accounted for by five publishers, and ten publishing firms accounted for more than 85%. Nine firms accounted for more than 50% of "general interest" book sales. The largest publishers in the country are Time, Inc., Gulf and Western, M.C.A., Times Mirror, Inc., The Hearst Corp., C.B.S. and Newhouse publications, conglomerates which all have heavy stakes in mass-market entertainment media, such as radio, book clubs, cable TV, pay TV, motion pictures, video discs, and paperback books. All of them have become significant factors only in the last ten years. (The general definition of oligopoly is an industry in which the eight largest firms have a 50 percent share of sales, and the largest 20 firms have at least 75 percent.)

Similar conglomeration can be noted in bookselling. In 1958, one-store "independent" book firms sold 72% of all books sold by booksellers. By 1981, the four largest bookstore chains approached 40 percent of sales, and it appears almost certain that this figure will have increased to 50 percent by the beginning of 1985.

trebled in less than a generation. Twenty years ago it took 2,500 copies @ $4-5.00 of a first novel to break even. Today the figure is at least 15,000 @ $11-15.00 (numbers which will be obsolete by the time this sees print). The effect of this is that the book buyer has seen his discretionary dollar devalued, so that he can buy one rather than four books.

Lit Law #3: *This audience simply has not increased exponentially with the increase in the cost of producing serious literature. Literature, in more than one sense, is a handmade art in a mass-production economy.*

This doesn't have the stink of a true conspiracy, only that of another technological system which doesn't work under pressure. Yet it is interesting how rather simple economic priorities gather unto themselves the most metaphysical of justifications. We are, of course, no longer talking about books but properties. But rarely do we hear this refreshing materialism any more. I have heard a vice-president of a large publishing house justify his reluctance to publish fiction by quoting George Steiner on the death of tragedy, Adorno on the impossibility of poetry in a world of concentration camps, McLuhan on the anality of print culture, and, finally, that crusher: TV has preempted the function of fiction. Of course it's quite true that fiction has lost its monopoly on middle-class consumer information — it lost that to the newspaper long before electricity. We are not being told that fiction is trying to tell us something different from the Evening News. We are being told that fiction represents an insufficient profit for those who also own the Evening News, that to survive at all it must be marketed like the Evening News, and that, as a matter of fact, the Evening News doesn't make that much money either.

Lit Law #4: *It is perhaps a little early to pronounce on the death of literature. What is certain is that publishing is less and less responsive to a pluralistic culture. Which can eventually amount to the same thing.*

For the moment, one ought to avoid drawing the obvious political implications from this analysis. We know that centralization of power will eventually involve censorship. But what is more important is that these corporate decisions are not wrong in terms of some high-flown aesthetics, so much as confused within their own logic, their own mythology of consumption.

Consider, for example, the remarks of Mr. Karl Fink before the American Institute of Graphic Arts:

> There are many ways . . . in which packaging could enhance the appeal of books — gift-wrapping keyed to special events, new types of groupings or sets, re-use features, user-oriented bindings and constructions, improved display of selling messages. But before such ideas can be tried on a realistic scale . . . attitudes of publishers toward the design and manufacture of their books must change. . . .
>
> They must learn to regard the book as a product to be packaged and sold as are other products, and they must develop, along with their manufacturers, a system of standardized alternatives to control today's undisciplined proliferation of physical variables.
>
> In applying to publishing the types of packaging thinking that takes place in other industries, the book must be viewed crassly as a product to be sold. Much as I respect literary merit and fine bookmaking, as a packager I must evaluate books in much the same way I evaluate a can of soup or a bottle of wine — as items which vie for consumer acceptance in order to make it in the marketplace. . . .
>
> There is, for instance, the matter of selling books in multiple units. I know that we have sets of Dickens or George Eliot or Winnie the Pooh, but what about grouping various books on one subject to develop multiple sales? Might not a travel guide to Spain be packaged with a road map, street maps of principal cities, a money changer, a tipping guide? Could not simultaneous publishing dates on Civil War books from different publishers be turned into enticing offerings — through joint packaging — to Civil War buffs, instead of competing for sales . . . ?
>
> And what about special-occasion packaging? We know that if you're looking for a Bible as a confirmation gift, there is a convenient choice between a white slipcover for girls and a simulated morocco for boys. But what about appealing covers encasing appropriate books for Mother's Day? Hearty barbecue books for Father's Day? Love poems for Valentine's Day? Graduation dictionaries?
>
> Still another packaging design staple that might be adapted to specialized books is the re-use container. The package for a book on birds might ultimately convert into a bird feeder. A cookbook's

binding might be doubled and hinged at the top to form its own easel.

We must find out more about people's attitudes toward books. Do they retain jackets or toss them away? If so, when? Do they dust books or leave them on shelves? Do they, in fact, keep them at all? Do they regard books as objects, as status symbols, or do they consider having read them the most important thing. . . .

[Publishers Weekly]

What's objectionable here is hardly Mr. Fink's indifference to intrinsic value. Indeed, he has struck an unwitting blow for concretism and paraliterature. The resistance of publishers to anything but the most standardized format has discouraged not only Mr. Fink but a good deal of innovative fiction, in the same way that the format of commercial magazines has had an undeniable if as yet unexamined effect not only on the content but the very structure of the American short story. Quality short fiction abounds. But whatever happened to the magazines which printed it? Again, the genre's evolution/reconstitution is confused with the demise of its traditional package or "vehicle." What is both saddening and hilarious is the desperate decision to submit all problems to repackaging. With so complex a product as books, packaging is the least efficacious way to solve a distribution problem. The failed solution of every commercial magazine to its structural economic problems in the last twenty years has been: (1) redesign format, (2) reduce trimsize, (3) cut back on fiction. Literature must retain considerable power if all those little stories are dragging entire corporations to fiscal ruin.

As long as the publishing industry subjects all of its products to the same promotional techniques, as long as serious books must compete not only with other books but with TV and gimmicks, and as long as literature remains undifferentiated from Confirmation gifts, its costs allocated according to the same overhead formulae, then of course its piececost will continue to rise and its claims on ordinary attention will continue to decrease.

Nevertheless, simple anti-commercialism can no longer be a unifying scapegoat. The university press, as self-advertised countervailing institution, has failed utterly to provide a genuine alternative press or distribution system. It has favored exegesis over art and generally ignored the culture of its time. It has not created a single innovation in production or distribution technology, despite massive subsidies and proximity to all the research facilities necessary. It has been timid editorially, conservative aesthetically, has failed to serve even the day-to-day educational needs of its own community (except to certify certain academic hiring and promotion policies) and ignored any audience beyond its narrowest constituency. It has passed its costs, in the form of outrageous prices, on to its basic consumer, the library, which in turn has passed them on to the government. And when the economic crunch comes, for the same reasons it has come to its commercial counterpart, the university press — rather than addressing itself to areas in which commercial publishers default, or acting as a subsidized countervailing institution — also loses its nerve. It too defines literature as marginal, so that the first things to go are the poetry series, the literary reviews, the search for the unexpected, all those "luxuries" whose constituency is never represented on policy-making boards. A strange situation: information which should be in retrieval systems, information which is of use only to a handful of specialists, is produced in thirty dollar limited editions; while literature, which not only has a wider potential audience, and whose only possible medium is the *book*, is ignored. The university press is as venally bound to a guaranteed library sale of specialist nonfiction as is a commercial publisher to its guaranteed sale on Greyhound bus station racks, and with the same results — the failure to cultivate an audience.

The first university press which puts its dissertations and statistical abstracts on microfilm, rethinks what ought to be *printed*, and devotes itself to the literature and the art of its time and place will make an indelible mark on this century, and perhaps even regain a measure of the respect for continuity and independent judgment which the university has forfeited.

Any assessment of the present literary situation must begin with the redefinition of "censorship" and "relevance," those sub-indices of free speech and intellectual freedom. It's quite clear, for example, that a commercial publisher can absorb criticism by pointing out its youth list, its woman's list, its black list. Indeed, when social issues are most polarized, it is perhaps easiest for the establishment to compartmentalize its market and to diffuse criticism with the illusion of contemporaneity. But the alacrity to cash in the literary chips on issues pre-glamorized by the media in no sense represents a more venturesome commitment to serious analysis or to the issues — a fact which Youth and Black culture have already found out, and as women will, when the returns start coming in. Nor does it have anything to do at all with either social relevance or literary innovation, which, in any case, have only the most tenuous relationship with each other.

Further, literary freedom has become equated almost solely with the license to use explicit language to describe sexuality, and in this case, the spread of pornography is seen as the last "breakthrough" in the fight for freedom of expression. It should be understood that the freedom to read or write "fuck" is directed more at the engorgement of the volume market than either the maximization of erotic desire or the elimination of constraint. Explicit sex, like explicit politics, has little to do with releasing the energies of serious literature. (Alas.) And such increased tolerance constitutes no Avant-Garde, only a middle-class acceptance of colloquial speech once limited to rare book and locker rooms.

In such a context, freedom of expression has come to mean little more than saying in public what was once formerly said or read in private, without frosty consequences. Most Americans understand cultural censorship as nothing more than bleeping talk shows, and literary censorship as a mouldering court battle won before they were born. (You don't, after all, need a Justice Brandeis when *Playboy* is apparently taking the fight right into the kitchenettes of America.)

Lit Law #5: *It doesn't matter what you say, or how you say it, but where. A classical totalitarian society censors at the production point. An oligopolistic democracy censors at the distribution point.*

A Modern government can kill off objectionable ideas with prurience or sedition laws, just as commercial publishing companies, by applying the same general overhead formulae to all its products, can limit minority reports. It is an instructive observation that countries with much more rigid official censorship laws — France and England, say —offer a better selection of serious literature to their consumers than the U.S.

What we are really talking about here are basic minority rights — the right to see one's efforts reach their widest possible audience. Serious fiction's constituency is not large — perhaps 100,000, at the very most, with 25,000 hard core. It is a minority which is at present nameless, and cannot organize beyond the ghostly images of electronic communication.

If a book deserves to be printed and is refused because it won't sell 10,000, that is censorship. If a novel is denied its potential audience because it is not reviewed, promoted, or in stock, that is censorship. It hardly matters whether this is due to ideological opposition, official ignorance, a conspiracy of indifference, or the exigencies of a "free" market, it has the same effect — the denial of a rightful audience and the loss of community. If we were told, for example, that an anti-establishment novel in Poland was printed in a small edition, went unpromoted and unreviewed, and then was rapidly allowed to go out of print and pulped, we would know the reasons why. Here, it happens every day, if for different reasons, and we are not scandalized. There is no fundamental difference between initially restricting information and making utterly unreasonable demands on the consumer. In fact, where censorship has a more bureaucratic structure, in Central Europe for example, a controversial play may be allowed to be printed but not performed, while a similar novel may be permitted to be read aloud at a club but not printed and circulated. There, censorship is effected *by denying the medium best suited to the form*. It has a familiar ring.

There are several reasons why we have not been able to develop a coherent theory of how America restricts literary as well as larger political options. The first is, of course, that we have relied on the European model of repression rather than really investigating the American tactic of absorption — the supermarket censors in its own way just as much as the ministry of culture. Intellectuals have never bothered to understand markets.

But even more importantly, the escalation of rhetoric — all sides accusing each other of being "dead" — has so banalized polemic that it is rare to see a telling attack upon the establishment, much less a genuine expression of agony. As Gerald Graff notes, "it used to be that one tried to prove one's enemies wrong. But now that right and wrong are 'meaningless' categories, it is better to identify the opposition as 'dead.' The Death Argument saves a lot of trouble because reasons are irrelevant; it is basically unanswerable, and it implies that the prosecutors are 'the lively ones.'"

The Leftist critique is even more irrelevant than usual. It tends to romanticize the older paternalistic, individualistic publishers, who in fact were gamblers because they had no other choice. To see the conflict as one between "workers" and "bosses," to be solved by "unionization," is totally to miss the uniqueness of conglomerate control, as well as the fact that the communications media represents the most powerful political and economic weapon of late capitalism, a sudden concentration of power which was not anticipated even by those who controlled it. To believe that the establishment systematically censors those who attack it, is simply to refuse reality. As the middle class absorbs Avant-Garde style, it is precisely the cheap anti-establishment product which is most promotable. The Left remains ineffective to the extent that it relies upon a classical theory of repression. It sees calculation and conspiracy where in fact there is only an open cynical indifference. To illustrate, consider this press release:

In response to an invitation to write a piece on "The Joy of Writing," James Purdy came up with the following put-on, which he obviously believed would never see the light of day.

In Observance of International Book Year
Observations
of American Writers

prepared by the Publishers Publicity
Association for reprint use in
newspapers and magazines

> In observance of International Book Year
> James Purdy, Author of "Elijah Thrush"
> published by Doubleday & Company, has
> written this personal observation on the
> American literary scene.

Writing from Inner Compulsion

I became a writer because there was no way for me to avoid writing, and I am in the same unchanged situation today. My early writings had to be privately printed because my work then as today violated the taboos and crotchets of the U.S. Publishing Monopoly (the taboos seem to change as the System goes on crumbling, but the main character of the monopoly remains — its outlawing of native vision and speech, it assassination of pure talent, and its denigration of integrity). Although over the years, beginning with my privately printed books on down to those of my writings which commercial publishers have condescended to publish, my readers may have increased by numbers, I am still writing from inner not outer compulsion, and my work is truly reaching only those few who can accept vision and voice

unconnected with the dogmatism of the politico-pornography
which constitutes American writing today.

I think that to be ignored by the vast collection of monopolies
which today control publishing, criticism, reviewing, the book
prizes, etc., to be swept, in fact, "under the rug," by this huge
structure, to be denigrated and isolated as I have been by it, far
from being 'hard luck' is in the end the best thing that could
happen to me or any other writer who has originality of vision
and tongue. Either one is a success and a copropragist in New
York, or he is out of it, sweetbreathed, and whole.

If one writes from inner prompting and the instinct to put down
his own voice on paper, he cannot expect rewards and accolades
from the most meretricious and deceitful, the most shoddy and
unreal civilization the world has ever seen.

This was of course printed and circulated as a fit "observation,"
despite its obvious disdain for the entire process, and it surely reached
a wider audience than Purdy's books. But there are several things in
the text worth remarking on. First, it is the writer placed in the position
of "cultural critic" once again, and note the extremity and rigidity of
the rhetoric — something Purdy would never permit himself in his
fiction. Also, whatever his indifference to "fame," there is an
underlying poignancy, the yearning for an audience. He knows very
well that what has happened to him is not the "best" thing; it is simply
preferable to being a clique's cutie or a hack. Indeed, like many
rebellious writers, he accepts the either/or criterion of success
promulgated by the industry; he simply reverses their valuation. But
Purdy's contradictions are less manifest than those of the industry which
can offer this wholesale condemnation of publishing as "publishers'
publicity," complete with a phone number to *Time-Life* Books. What
possible follow-up could they offer? What other culture would bother
to absorb the most vitriolic attack, repackage it, and cynically throw
it back in the face of the writer as an instance of their indifference?
This sort of strangulated fury is what is expected from the writer, this
is what comes of "writing from inner compulsion," this is the writer's
real *role* because it can be written off to the rhetoric of the alienated —
specialists in the last gasp. And because Purdy has nothing to fall back
on save the dubious integrity of his isolation, the Publishers' Publicity
Association knows that these words, no matter how true or sick, are
no threat to them. Or perhaps — and this is the most terrifying aspect

of this artifact — perhaps we are so accustomed to such self-pitying rhetoric that it is impossible to give it any credence. It exists only as a mirror image of somnambular Time/Speak: *nil admirari, nil desperandum*.

What we are dealing with here is the preemption by the media of the writer as *celebrity*. The talk show is, after all, an attempt to create through instantaneous exposure what was once mythology or at least romantic rumor. At least people could genuinely envy Hemingway or sympathize with Fitzgerald, for these writers' self-promotion was related directly to the authentication of their art; their posturing was a way of testing the reality of their narrators as well as their audience, and we should suffer little nostalgia over this. After all, it's demonstrably destructive for writers to live out the attenuated fantasies of the public; they should rather be read than recognized. We have grown up to the extent that we can see that artists might have other serious social roles besides that of the celebrity *functionaire*. In this sense, literature has certainly become de-prophetized, and the only societies in which a writer can still claim traditional charisma are those in which the government either officially honors its writers or punishes them publicly with 19th century authoritarian *élan*. It is hard to imagine an American government getting around to doing either.

But the key determinant in understanding the uneasy relationship of literary culture to the general culture is the failure to make the technology of bookmaking responsive to a pluralistic culture. The most powerful idea to come out of the 20th century American experiment was the transfer of an Enlightenment view of political life to culture itself. For if our politics have been basically conservative, it is in the operation of our cultural and artistic life that our more radical ideals have had their greatest expression. Against the European notion of culture as *standards* enforced by an elite, we have come to see culture as a series of unexpected alternatives, and the greatest legacy of the otherwise dissipated radical politics of the sixties (as well as the greatest oversight of the liberal mind) was the realization that the communications structure must be challenged before you can hope to alter, much less bind, thought and action.

When the economy of scale appropriate to mass culture is applied to a more selective and complex print culture, inelastic contradictions between the production and transmission of art emerge. In an inflationary era, the conglomerate requires larger and larger rates of return to justify its risk in a volatile market, and, more importantly, *only* the conglomerate can afford to capitalize upon a market so distorted. Power in an inflationary climate is defined as unlimited access to short term credit at whatever cost, and the ability to pass on costs with impunity.

Modernism hitched its star to enlightened paternalistic patronage — which self-destructed long before the mass entertainment industry increased its sway. In this sense Modernist writers never acknowledged the extent to which they were dependent upon the traditional social relations which they were hell bent on destroying. Though Post Modernism *intellectually* moves more easily — some would say too easily — between high and mass culture, it has never come to terms with the *processes* of capitalist consumer culture in an inflationary era. Its intellectual spokesmen generally refuse to see that alienation has a practical and historical basis, that it masks uneasy affiliations between the intelligentsia and the corporate world, and that the forces which affect the transmission of art are no different from those which affect the political economy as a whole. In this sense the struggle of the publishing industry is a convenient social metaphor. When it became efficacious for individual firms to sell out to conglomerates, the conventional inflationary wisdom was to maximize and releverage short term cash flow, reduce marginal enterprises, maximize income from "blockbusters," and pass on ever-increasing costs to the consumer. This had the effect of only intensifying the secular trend of downgrading long term planning and reinvestment. Inflation exacerbated the situation in the by now familiar pattern: the bureaucratic structure is expanded, long term contracts and relationships are invalidated, editors and writers change affiliation almost randomly, increasingly shoddy merchandise proliferates, and keeping "marginal" books in print, or printing them in the first place, becomes highly unprofitable. As a result, serious literature disappears from the marketplace.

Lit Law #6: *The audience for serious literature cannot be consistently reached by conventional marketing devices, no matter how intensively applied.*

In other words, the present system cannot cater to the reflective, selective buyer who is most likely to be primarily impressed by word of mouth, occasionally a review, and the actual physical presence of the book. The answer to this — as with all such problems of quality items in competition with the mass market — is selectivity, lower cost, and proximity to minority consumers; which means, fewer copies of a wider spectrum of books in a larger and more varied number of outlets — exactly the reverse of the present situation.

The intellectual tends to see conglomeration only in terms of traditional centralized power, which he assumes to have an ideological motivation and coherence (the only kind of power he chooses to understand, because it is the only kind he can rebel against), and he also assumes that corporate deviousness is based on cleverness. He does not understand how insidiously inflationary assumptions can unsettle the most self-interested and economically successful, nor how long it takes market excesses to self-correct. Moreover, he does not see how in inflation finance develops into an autonomous sector of its own, only tenuously connected to the actual productive economy, and how little concerned conglomerate management is with the actual functions of its various subsidiaries. Post-Modern finance constitutes the Formalism of the Real World.

The fact of the matter is that the trade book industry was never efficient to the extent that it was subsidized by paperback subsidiary rights. The success of the mass market paperback only proved one thing — that the capacity of the market to absorb a large variety of books is there. Seduced by unprecedented subsidiary income, trade book publishing experienced the distorted valuation and volume of an inflationary explosion — overselling, overpaying, overprinting and overpricing. When these excesses were magnified by a sluggish economy, paperback houses found that they could no longer cover advances much less increase profits. The process of mechanical replication which Walter Benjamin thought infinitely sustainable had its market limitations. What appeared to be cyclical change was in fact structural change, and capitalists are no better at distinguishing between the two than anyone else.

If corporate self-interest were really as efficient as intellectuals think it is, it would not have lost its control over its own mechanisms of distribution. By allowing its traditional independent outlets to die out, the publishing conglomerates in fact created the bookchains as well as their present business relationship with them, which is essentially one of unspoken blackmail.

The irony of the conglomerates' takeover is of course that they moved into publishing, cut the heart out of it, and are now trying to unload the firms as fast as they acquired them. There is no evidence that conglomerates brought any new relevant managerial, technological or marketing skills to their new enterprises. An accounting mentality and retrenchment can only help in the short run; it cannot respond to a structural crisis. There seem to be some modest lessons here:

> Print media cannot compete with television by making books into "total entertainment" packages with innumerable tie-ins and spinoffs. The market will not prosper unless the intrinsic properties of the product are respected.

> Trade book publishing must seek its own threshold. This means reinvestment in product so that backlist accounts for a much larger percentage of income. (In the last decade, backlist income has fallen from 70% to 30% as a percentage of net income.)

> Risk cannot be reduced in the long run by cutting back on the quality of product. It probably makes good business sense to respect the pluralism of the culture with a greater diversity of product.

Whether publishing will be able to readjust to these realities in an era of disinflation remains an open question. It will be interesting to see what happens to publishing when it concedes that it simply cannot manage a rate of return comparable to parallel industries. A return to a smaller scale is not out of the question. The problem with publishing is not that it is autarchic but that it has become in the context of its corporate ownership a peripheral and even risky investment.

It is nevertheless possible that literature may require what every other surviving mode of creative expression has had in any culture under any system, namely subsidy — its own house in which it can cultivate its audience. In a country as large and diverse as ours, where both talent and need are rarely concentrated, this would seem a necessity even if the economics were less deterministic and did not threaten to get worse.

What happened to serious fiction only happened to it first. As the art form with the least organized constituency, it was the first to feel the effects of inflation and the fragmentation of audience. The repertory theatre has met the same fate, as has the general-interest magazine. There remains not a single quality periodical or repertory theatre in America which is not massively subsidized. This shift in priorities which began with the reallocation of the advertising dollar to television now affects even the most deeply entrenched institutions, the academic humanities and quality daily newspapers. The banal fact is that over the last twenty years, we have suffered an unprecedented deterioration in the agencies which transmit print culture, a fact masked by the rhetoric of linguistic alienation.

Last Lit Law: *Just as publishing is the last consumer industry to recognize the shift in emphasis from production to a distribution economy, so literature remains the last serious art form which has any pretensions about paying its own way in the mass market place.*

Now it may be legitimately asked, how can you extrapolate from what happens to some unworldly jerk's first novel to the political economy as a whole? And how is it that if the demand for fiction is decreasing, its costs and prices keep rising, since all conventional economic wisdom dictates that inflation is caused by excess aggregate demand? The reasons are crushingly simple, reflecting a failure of understanding equivalent to that which led to the Great Depression, and they explain why the standard Adversary critique of the liberal intellectual is no longer taken seriously by anyone.

Intellectuals, Marxist or no, are fixated on the concepts of monopoly and conspiracy, good Modernist notions. Like all people corrupted by the lack of power, they envision authority as controlling supply through secret agreement, subject to restraint only by demand of competitive markets.

But every seller constitutes a monopoly to the degree that he has the power to increase prices without affecting sales, and such pricing institutions are not on the whole undesirable, as pure price competition would be totally disruptive of the economy. The peculiar distortion of inflation is caused by the temporary predominance of a seller's monopoly, and the fact that inflationary assumptions are so deeply embedded in the social fabric that collusion is unnecessary. The confusion arises because the liberal intellectual uncritically accepts the deterministic supply and demand theory of competitive markets as an accurate description of actual conditions; his caveat is only that "actual conditions" do not take into account aspects of the culture which cannot be measured in monetary terms, and thus intervention is required.

His critique, in other words, is based upon the assumption of truly competitive markets and complete monopoly. So the question is not one of whether or not the model provides social justice, but what, in actual fact, prevents the market from clearing itself. *Nothing* influences social and political behavior more than markets which do not establish equilibrium.

Modernist social and political assumptions are simply irrelevant to understanding oligopolistic markets in an inflationary age. For what defines an oligopoly is not so much its unconstrained power, but the impossibility of determining a theory of price from its operation. And price theory is precisely where the interventionist takes issue, since any theory of *value* and its implicit moral and social concerns is directly derived from a notion that there exists a mechanism for determining fair price.

Oligopoly has historically prevented prices from falling by not passing on the savings technologically attainable cost reductions ordinarily permit; it responds to inflation by reducing output. Indeed, falling demand in such a system may result in price increases, if by underutilization of capacity it raises unit costs; in other words, an oligopoly may raise prices simply to avoid incurring a loss. In the past, inflation was controlled because underutilization of resources would eventually force prices down. But in contemporary inflation, underutilization is a constant factor; it cannot be "used up," because every time excess capacity is reduced, inflation flares up.

Further, to the extent that the Adversary argument is based upon the presumption of acquisitiveness and affluence, it loses its force if an oligopoly's profits can be concealed in paper transfers, or if they are in fact non-existent. If there are no profits, the question of their redistribution or reinvestment becomes irrelevant. The Left is in disarray for precisely the same reasons the Avant-Garde has become diffused —the nature of the "enemy" has changed. Having based its opposition upon the rapacity of single-minded self-interest and effective exploitation, it is difficult for the Left suddenly to shift and accuse "them" of timidity, confusion and downright incompetence.

The conventional Adversary stance not only confuses older monopolistic manipulation with the more subtle and effective oligopoly; it refuses to see how the mentality of the seller's monopoly suffuses the entire culture, not by some secret agreement, but through tacit emulation and sheer ignorance. To take the most obvious example, in an economy increasingly oriented to services, the manner in which college tuitions are set differs in no important way from the manner in which corporate law firms set their fees. "Professionals" enter the field and practice in subordinate relationships to those already established, rather than competing with them, handing over a large portion of the general fees for the privilege of practicing through an established outlet. The result is that the consumer cannot judge either the quality of services or the appropriateness of the fees charged. If you want a metaphor for Post-Modern alienation, you need not dredge up existential plaints or linguistic determinism, but simply take note that the audience in an inflationary era has increasingly little way of determining the *value* of anything it wants or needs. Inflation renders obsolete the very notion of voluntary exchange, as both buyer and seller are under the pressure of an anticipated price rise. No positivist method can measure the complexity of motive here, nor the psychological damage inflicted by such collective uncertainty.

In short, supply and demand, whether you are for it or against it, is no longer an adequate model, if it ever was, to explain an economy which no longer attempts to stimulate demand through price reduction. As W. David Slawson, among others, has demonstrated, contemporary inflation is primarily caused not by excess demand or lessened competition, monetary policy or government spending (though these all may contribute) but by inflationary assumptions anticipated by the entire culture. The social order becomes engaged in a vast competitive battle of group against group for a share of the aggregate income, a war in which prices are set by non-price competition, which include advertising, barriers to entry, and new product development. This gives the illusion that demand is not slackening because everybody's prices are creeping upward together, and accounts for the fact that in the later stages of inflation, the emphasis of necessity is to concentrate primarily on the "upscale" market. The first audience lost to booksellers is blue collar. In a single generation, we have seen the book transformed *back* into a cultural luxury.

The important thing here is not to be deluded that we have a situation amenable to a little good will and technical correction. The question is how to reassert the pride of independent artisans, which has up to now been the false pride (resentment) of metaphysical or linguistic isolation, and to demand a reorganization of priorities without adopting some facile paranoia. This is asking, obviously, for a lot more sour grapes, but nothing could be worse than the present combination of alienation and smugness which attends the activity of *making* books. It is about time the American writer ceased confusing his peripherality with freedom of expression, and began to find out where he fits into productive and social relations of the world which most affects him. He will undoubtedly be told that the price of his concern will be his imagination; that his job is to stay in his room and write, write, write; that his "time will come." If a twelve-year-old Puerto Rican kid in a ghetto can understand this brand of paternalism, you would think a literate adult might.

This argument is embarrassing because most everyone would agree with it and no one knows what to do about it. It is not a lofty ventilation; it lacks deep theory and detachment; its technical aspects date with each change in the financial markets. But it does not suppose that literature, writers or their audience can be improved by throwing money at them; it merely takes into account that literature does require an arena, a material and intracultural context, which is swiftly being eroded, not by some vague aesthetic malaise, some sublime bifurcation between sensation and language, but by economic and political realities of the "communications" industry, about which every thinking person in the culture is passively disgusted. The efforts which will be necessary to make the system responsive are unprecedented. It is one thing to overthrow the Viennese Academy, quite another to reform CBS. Avant-garde posturing will not suffice. The aim is simply to reaffirm that there are ways of producing and of experiencing art which occupy that immense and pleasurable space between belletristic coterie and mass market hype.

It is easy enough, after all, to blame venal businessmen, who have no monopoly on uncertainty. What is more depressing is that there is nothing in American intellectual life to suggest a coming to grips with the problem. There is an absolute unwillingness to examine the apparatus through which the artist is threaded. And if the intellectual can so ill-perceive the single instance of external cultural authority which affects him professionally, how can he claim *any* understanding of a political nature? The fact of the matter is that Post-Modern intellectuals have not behaved like disenfranchised, detached or unemployed persons, but rather as an entrenched service class which provides increasingly little service. They have responded to inflation like any other substratum of the middle class — that is, in terms of its own short term occupational and life-style interests, a radically self-interested attitude which is nothing more than a vast competitive struggle to protect its present position from further erosion.

Any partial solution will strike at the most unexamined notions of the culture, recognizing that "communications" are too important to be considered just another conventional profit-center; that much of what is most important to the long term benefit of the culture cannot survive, much less advance, when subjected to the high-cost technology and financial stakes of the high-rolling conglomerate out for the short term return. Nothing will be accomplished until the inflationary context of short term profit is redefined.

If the literary community is to survive it must reconstitute itself, not in terms of a stylized adversary but by recovering its own structural integrity. No act of isolated individual genius, no authoritative figure or unitary theory of culture, can accomplish this. In a time when the intellectualization of a society seems to go hand in hand with the bureaucratization of culture, and the Academy has failed utterly as an alternative to commercialism, except to exploit it as a unifying scapegoat, it is difficult for any writer to have much faith in any reinstitutionalization of literature.

Literary and even print culture is now a minority culture, not by some elitist manifesto but by economic and social definition. An adversary culture, even a hypocritical one, requires a periphery in which to operate, and that periphery becomes squeezed to the vanishing point in the climax stages of inflation. The advances of literacy are behind us, and literary art, which has ridden the bowed back of education since World War II, will have to find other forms of perpetuation. It is obvious that no one has thought very seriously about what forms this will take.

We have barely survived the two organizational myths of the 20th century: that entrepreneurial impulse will solve all problems if only left unfettered, and that the failure of the market utopia can be solved by turning all planning over to the state. No one can argue any longer that capitalism is synonymous with freedom of expression, *or* that state ownership would be more humanizing. In one sense, the corporate conglomerate has been a pragmatic compromise between these extremes, and we should not be surprised that it has been vulnerable to the same confusion, smugness and self-aggrandizement which beset other institutions (political and academic, for instance) not so thoroughly committed to the bottom line. In this situation, the kind of institution in which literary art might again flourish suggests a form of organization which might well serve other aspects of social value.

Perhaps some new breakthrough in technology will relegate our complaints to insipidity, or perhaps disinflation will restore a fresh if circumscribed meaning to literary culture. Perhaps a new politics will produce men who see language as having a more precisely instrumental relationship to behavior. Or perhaps we will become totally habituated to the media and allowed to truly die, having, as Thoreau put it, at least the pleasure of "hearing the rattle of our throats and cold in the extremities."

But even then would we be considered Mandarins, a minority clinging to a sincere if exhausted impulse? Or simply part of the voting majority who panicked in the face of a clogged horizon?

24. The Permanent Crisis Unsprung

> *Until now, philosophers kept the solution of all mysteries inside their desks, and the stupid uneducated world merely had to open its mouth and the fried dove of Absolute knowledge would fly in. Philosophy is now secular, for which the best proof is that philosophical consciousness itself feels the pain of the struggle not merely externally, but also internally. It is not our task to construct the future and to deal with everything once and for all, but it is clear what we have to do at present — I am thinking of the* merciless criticism of everything that exists — *merciless criticism in the sense that it is not afraid of its findings, and just as little afraid of conflict with the existing powers . . . It will be found that what is involved is not to draw a large dash between past and future, but to realize* the ideas of the past . . . *it will be found that humanity does not start a new task, but consciously carries through the old.*
>
> *— Marx to Ruge, 1843*

It's perhaps best simply to conclude with some assertions and take the consequences.

For reasons which are not abundantly clear, there have evolved two currently opposed notions about what narrative literature ought to be. These cannot profitably be associated with individual writers, any more than with seminal idea structures — they constitute collective and largely unconscious mental habits, reactions which appear unique to our age, but are nevertheless historically conditioned. The first and presumably "new" notion is that fiction can no longer be concerned with processing and disseminating information about "how we live," particularly for its traditional audience, the middle class, that its subject matter is essentially the endless interrogation of its own artifice, that it cannot but be acutely aware of both its precursors and its own ongoing activity. Curiously enough, this self-consciousness generally reflects itself in the self-effacement of the author as *personality*. While the author may constantly intrude, *qua* author, it is rarely in an autobiographical or confessional manner. At the same time, the underlying momentum of such fiction is achieved by reminding the reader that the work is putting distance between itself and its literary antecedents, an obligatory if occasionally conscience-stricken break with the past, in particular that peculiarly reified past known as "Modernism." This historical isolationism is further heightened by the novel's effort to differentiate itself from its popular counterpart; any concession to mass appeal is incorporated only as satire.

Such writing is highly. polished, as concerned as poetry once was with the weight of each sentence, word, and for that matter, ellipsis; indeed it claims every province which was once poetry's exclusively, while cultivating a critical obsession with its own legitimacy. Insofar as it acknowledges *any* audience, it often intimidates it in both a practical and metaphysical sense: often such reflexive works can be read not merely as an act of contempt but even an act of hatred against the reader (or perhaps the absence of not only an *ideal* but *any* reader). In its suspicion of its audience, it exudes misgivings about its own procedure, and evolves a curiously antagonistic strategy, which is something much more powerful than the mere unwillingness to yield itself up to recognizable narrative conventions. It is elitist without being hierarchical, intellectual without being high-minded, a cerebration which its opponents accuse of lacking either compelling situation or release.

The humor of this fiction is primarily parodic, its form frequently trades on fable or instant myth; its fragmentation is programmatic, its archness almost always stops short of pathos. It is fiercely dedicated to the integrity of autonomous verbal expression, and stands four square against the extra-literary pressures which have always surrounded fiction as a genre. It recognizes that its basic resources are irreparably, and without apology, literary. Above all, this writing is concerned with language, if not as the creator of reality, then as the ultimate shaper of consciousness. It is never framed by a dominant outside reality, and it thus tends eventually to reduce all distinctions to linguistic ones, exemplifying both temporal and historical subjectivity. It is radical aesthetically, largely apolitical and ahistorical, and in its relation of even the most terrifying matters, purportedly value-free.

When this writing works, it reminds us how remarkably flexible Anglo-Saxon prose can be, how relentlessly innovative American fiction of the last twenty years has been, and what a young, unexplored, and wonderfully hybrid tradition we have been permitted to explore. When it is really good we are reminded that this commodity we hold in our hands is somehow more alive than we are; that *reference* seems almost beside the point.

When it doesn't work we are reminded that innovation in and of itself is not only tedious but ultimately self-cancelling, that what we finally want from literature is neither amusement nor edification, but the demonstration of a real authority which is not to be confused with sincerity, and of an understanding which is not gratuitous. We are reminded how easy it is for writers to imitate themselves, how cleverness can get you out of almost any contemporary confrontation; how tempting it is to write a book that is *teachable* rather than memorable without prosthetic devices. We are reminded that irony, no matter how many-layered, is not inherently sufficient to get any book through its night — any more than those great crosshatched loaves of "manners" were, or those sententious psychological certainties which once fully assimilated human character. Finally, it appears that it is not the best strategy to have as a central premise of one's book that better books exist.

Another very different kind of contemporary fiction is frequently written by people who view the established culture as something more than a set of aesthetic conventions to be called in for questioning. What is most obvious here is that while this writing is overtly political, historical in a revisionist sense, unabashedly concerned with how we ought to live, it is conventional and often even boorish in its aesthetics. It certainly assigns technical virtuosity and sophistication a lower priority in its procedures. It is not under the obligation to dispense with historically certified aesthetic baggage — indeed, its ideology often dismisses the Modernist tradition as either obscurantist or irrelevant. It sees no contradiction in trading upon the formulae of popular fiction while putatively opposing its content, often creating an art indistinguishable from those bourgeois forms it ideologically despises, without irony or self-consciousness. It attacks the reader's social prejudices but not his linguistic competence. It refuses both poetic effect and critical theorizing, tends to equate anti-elitism with realism, and rejects any pose of autonomy. It grants fewer aesthetic margins yet presupposes a greater intimacy between reader and writer, and whatever its commitments, they are constantly on display.

The opposing and energizing notion of this Neo-Realism is that there is *new* information which is not made redundant by other media, information which does not have to be "made up," but rather is shaped or *aimed*, because such substantive experience has been repressed, neglected or distorted. More importantly, this notion of literature often presupposes a receptive audience which has a special need for this information, a collective unconscious which in fact awaits collection.

As opposed to the writers of the first group who flaunt their futility and isolation, advertising as redundant survivors in a world where literary life consists largely of amnesiacal anecdotes, this second group of writers offer themselves as "spokespersons," often in an unabashedly autobiographical manner. Indeed, they often claim access to experience presumably unavailable to the imagination *in vacuo*, a socially specific experience which cannot be understood (or judged) by those outside their constituency.

When this sort of writing works, we are reminded how difficult it is to do that basic thing, to *move* a reader in this strange unvisceral transaction, how small are the advances that have been achieved in the brief and anomalous history of fiction, how no literature of any age has ever lived up to its own extra-literary rhetoric. When it works, we are reminded that perhaps the most unusual act of a modern writer is not to overthrow one's father's forms, but to write about one's own time and place without self-consciousness, recognizing simultaneously how fast our particular culture dates us, and how the very consumption patterns which gain us a moment of visibility consign us just as quickly to the periphery of the honored and unread. This used to be the experience of "older" writers who simply went "out of style." It is now experienced by the vast majority of "living authors" whose texts are erased by the declining return on investment. In an inflationary environment, the rate of obsolescence increases exponentially.

When it is bad we are reminded how often what seemed "secret" information is nothing more than conventional wisdom unworthy of relation, how easy it is to confuse our own desperate lives with the disparate history of our time; that the fact that we are suffering unspeakably does not have in it the shape of a book, that simple justice has unfortunately not much to do with art, and that the impulse to write has nothing intrinsically noble about it whatsoever. It reminds us, finally, that it is questionable strategy consciously to construct a work of literature with indifference to its literary elements.

It is no secret that the first kind of writing often takes a more academically acceptable form, while the latter tends to be communal and even commercial, at least in fits and starts. But it is worth noting that *both* groups tend to view themselves as rebellious, if not revolutionary. Both pose as *the* vanguard, and both present themselves in aggressively absolutist rhetoric. It would not be surprising if our literary era were labelled by future critics as *The Age of Overkill*. Here we have a dim echo of the contest between speech and the written word. Against the Formalism of a style which in its originality refuses an invitation to the audience is opposed a notion of pure speech of the "people," who are dispossessed and enslaved by those who assert the superiority of a written language. In both cases, this is adolescent fantasy. It is as if the only way to challenge the precocity of Formalism is to politicize everything, so that technique becomes something which is *lost* when writing opens itself up to the broader ranges of experience.

What we end up with is a dichotomy which does not pit technique against technique, or vision against vision, but technique against vision. Nothing could be more indicative of our cultural disarray than this hysterical alternation between the impulse to stop art and reload it with some solid moral or psychological function and the impulse to redeem art from servitude to those very powers, the grotesquely confused and superlatively vague false dualism between life-enhancement and art-alarms, which indicates only a loss of the primary appetites for both art and life. And if one wishes to *debate* the question, one can argue either side with equal authority, just as a physicist can teach wave theory on Tuesday and particle theory on Thursday.

And yet, and yet, for all the brute recalcitrance of this finally inane dialectic, those contemporary writers who have not acknowledged their struggle with it seem to have half the world hidden from them.

This false hypostatizing of the operative worlds of Formalism and Realism further degenerates into a subspecies of argument which might be called the "right to live" people *versus* the "right to write" people — a regurgitation of the "cooked v. uncooked" debate emergent in poetry during the fifties, which has had not much lasting effect except in the culinary industry. If it is impossible to have much sympathy with those who insist that what we need is *more* deliberate incoherence in our literature in order to remind us that reality is made up as we go along (a perception which is hardly new, and is in fact the literary basis of the Declaration of Independence), neither can we go along with those who declare as a professional matter that literature exists to remind us that the world is made up of "mere" words, and that life had better understand this elemental matter, or else.

A case can certainly be made against the easily purchased surrealism, willful randomness and cheap narrative collage so characteristic of Post-Modern literature. There is no such thing as randomness in literature; randomness is simply a sequence which is predetermined to be undetermined. But such a case has not yet been made by those who pronounce themselves in the Wake of The Main Stream, who project a Realist didacticism as perverse as the hand-me-down know-nothingism of the Avant-Garde. Arguments for a "literature for life" are, in this context, invariably self-serving and transparent apologies for popularization, just as self-concerned as the most logocentric of authors. Why is it that books which purport to tell us "how to live" bring out our most homicidal instincts? And why is it that claims for a "magic" realism are invariably couched in such insolently unpolished mush? It is because in literature, the power of the unrepressed is not achieved through the refusal to make elementary revisions.

Realism of course always presents a tougher philosophical problem than the most scholastic Formalism. Technique can be shared more easily than reality, since every time you try to step back from realism in any historical era, you only insure that "reality" steps forward. Such are the breaks of mediation.

The present situation suggests a few behavioristic rules which ought to be viewed not as cynicism but as genuine and healthy limitations of intelligence.

1. If a writer thinks of himself as an experimentalist he is responsible to the scientific sense of that metaphor, is accountable for his findings, and ought not simply throw the

results of his investigations into the face of the audience. "How long," Breton asked, "are such idiots worth working over?"

2. If a writer proclaims himself as *avant garde* he cannot rely on the tautological argument that the avant garde is what's happening now, and since we're what's happening now, therefore we're the avant garde. He is responsible for delineating that race of which he claims to be the antennae. He is also probably mistaken to take the periphery so much for granted, or to think of the Void as a fat pitch over the inside corner.

3. If a writer announces the Death of Literature and the Debasement of Language in the Reign of Silence, he should have the good sense to practice what he preaches and re-evaluate his career objectives.

4. If a writer lays claim to a tradition of the Universal Verities of human experience, he has the responsibility to give them concrete particularization, and to face the question of whether the eternal bears repeating. This does not mean, however, that he is enjoined to rely upon traditonal psychology, sociology or dramaturgy to create a "traditional" voice. Human experience is not Humanism and Humanism is not those disciplines certified by the Academy.

5. If a writer proclaims himself as isolated, uninfluenced and responsible to no one, he should not be surprised if he is ignored, uninfluential and perceived as irresponsible.

6. And, finally, if a writer presumes to speak from within a *new* collective consciousness, a reconstructed language and specialized experience, he has the responsibility to distinguish what is really first-rate in this emerging community. Nothing kills a legitimate movement faster than the failure to develop a principle of rigorous internal self-criticism, which is the first lesson of 20th century revolutionism.

The unexceptional debate between those whose message is form and those for whom form has distorted message testifies to an art *in extremis*: so does the entire ludic litany of the Death of Art and Absence of Meaning which is only underscored by the appeal to a rebirth of the real in its most sentimental and shopworn guise: the restoration of the currency by counterrevolution, Formalist sovereignty refurbished with Literal Revivalism.

We tend to forget how much Bourgeois realism the Modernists were able to incorporate into their activity of attacking it, and more importantly how inadequate is the adversarial stance of Modernism toward a culture dominated not by petit Bourgeois Academic Classicism, but by the mass entertainment industry and the democratized university, two powerful mediating institutions, neither of which is anticipated in the Modernist tradition.

The real irony of Modernism blindly carried forward is that it continues to attack the pretensions of a conservative, print-oriented culture, the kind of plodding, judgmental, sequential, standardized interpretive manners which, in fact, have disappeared. Ours is the Age of Narration, but it is based upon instantaneous pattern recognition, not delayed analytic decoding.

Post-Modernism carries out the aesthetics of anti-realism in an external fashion, while rejecting the varieties of Modernism in both its extreme Transcendent and Nihilistic modes. Its peculiar tone is dictated by the conflict between the remnants of Bourgeois realism and an anti-Bourgeois epistemology — a pervasive skepticism about skepticism as the ultimate formulation of art. No doubt this requires the gestures of autonomy, but it is an autonomy which is no longer voluntary, and without content. To paraphrase Mallarmé: one must be employed before one can strike.

Is there an antidote to the complacent and sacerdotal Post-Modern irony, this smug and snug slipperiness which trades upon ambivalence and chiliasm and sells it back at cost plus 10%? History is an accumulative process which does not allow strategic retreats to simpler ways, but if an aesthetic structure no longer serves its original purpose, is it necessary to rip it out entire? One can perhaps do this with peasant economies, but not with art forms. Our current rhetoric almost always prefers the analeptic to the polysemic — we think in terms of "restoring" value rather than acquiring new meaning which amplifies the old. This is the crisis mentality fostered by cultural inflation at its most damaging; the value of all real goods is discounted in advance.

There is indeed a place for a realistic impulse directed to a traditional concern with the secrets embedded in the social fabric. We live in a time of unprecedented multiple overlapping ideologies and vocabularies; special regional, psycho-social and even biological gender interests, as compartmentalized and concrete as the class system upon which the 19th century novel capitalized. Technological society calls forth a new Balkanized social order and specialized short-lived languages which require decoding. It is Post-Modernism's special default that it generally parodies these languages and leaves it at that. Jargon is too important to be left to the Comic. As Adorno says, "History does intrude on every word and withholds each word from the recovery of some alleged original meaning, that meaning which the jargon is always trying to track down." This particular challenge is always with the artist whether he likes it or not. As James Baldwin puts it: "nothing, I submit, *nothing* is more difficult than deciphering what the citizens of this time and place *actually* feel and think." "One is always faced with the difficulty," Henry James concludes, "of collecting evidence which is so far from being purely literary."

The phony dualism between Formalism and Realism, and the tortuous idolatries of style it inspires, are only the most boring and insidious of the collective confusions of the age, to which no one is immune. With Bellow, Barthelme, and Gass, three remarkable writers writing out of three utterly different traditions, traditions which in effect they have invented, the dialectic still retains tension. As the epigoni succeed one another, it degenerates into total gesture. How to account, for example, for the continued obsession with autonomy, which denies any reciprocity between genres, style and idea, literature and society, or the writer and the reader? Partly, it is the Formalist bias which still so powerfully underlies so much contemporary endeavor. Certainly "common experience" has been disrealized and vulgarized, to the extent that we now characterize any small change in our lives as "learning experiences." We know that the media oversimplifies ideas; what is often overlooked is that every *feeling* which has one iota of legitimacy is also trivialized. Contemporary literature reflects not so much a superabundance of intellect as a visceral timidity, which no theory of repression can adequately convey. No one would dare begin a serious work of criticism today as Nietzsche did: "I am at all costs going to venture on a description of *my feelings* . . ." Formalism in such a circumstance often retreats not so much to the fantastic, but to the compositional. It becomes suspect when it refuses the experience of *knowing*. It comes to reflect, not the superiority of the technically refined, but a wounded and weakened ego, the guilt and rage of withdrawal, a cloudbank from which issues the S.O.S.: *Fiction Sinking, Sentence Saved.*

There is more to fiction than fiction. To discover that there is no experience without language is not blithely to assume that language is divorced from experience. When Formalism becomes self-ironic and facetious, masquerading as "pure style," the hypocrisy of mimeticism is cancelled out by the fatuity of form as final consolation.

An uncontested formalism, then, has pushed the truly original in our time into the clichés of a hopelessly derivative innovation, every man able to acquire his piece of chaos, sold off as remnants of figureless carpet from the great discount warehouse of classic European Modernism. These are the clichés codified by the Second Revolution, parrotted by every theoretician who, running out of categories and dumbfounded by the redundancy of dialectical methods, piously falls back on the "modern virtues" of dislocation and indeterminacy. What is overlooked of course is that in an inflationary culture the center is always dispersed; more, it is popular culture which has achieved the monopoly on iconoclasm, with the result that serious art is engaged in the constant annexation of a "new territory," whether suitable for development or not. Milieu moves at mature mach speeds, with character following like a peasant on a bicycle. It may well be, as any *Arts and Leisure* section in the morning newspaper will tell us, that we are stimulated not by art which "confirms our sense of the world," but by that which "challenges it." But the true mystery of contemporary experience is not that the artist lacks the means to play the game of "challenge," but that no one can tell us exactly what it is that "confirms our sense of the world."

In short, art has become indexed to cultural inflation, and the only risky thing about art in such a context is to possess an asset which is not subject to irrational speculative bidding. It is no accident, then, that the deterministic clichés of our time are above all *perceptual*, the most impermeable ideology yet devised, in which the artist must always provide "new ways of seeing," and that such "sight" dominates and determines the external world. Taken far enough, this exempts artists from having to produce ideas, values, methods, or judgment. And it is equally handy for the consumer, for it provides him with an all-purpose rejoinder: "it all depends on your point of view"; meaning, of course, that he has no point of view.

This enthronement of the perceiver is of course only the most egregious Humanist misreading of Modern physics, which ignores not only the elegant and excruciating step-by-step methodology which characterizes the true scientific method, but also the horror which always accompanies the discovery of new evidence which cannot be explained in an old context. The point of course is that when Werner Heisenberg told us that the nature of phenomena is affected by the bias of the perceiver, he did not mean that the perceiver creates the world, but that a new angle of perception always conceals as much as it reveals. In this context, it is instructive to listen to the father of the "uncertainty principle" on the history of his discovery.

> . . . at no time during the history of the quantum theory was there a physicist or a group of physicists seeking to bring about an overthrow of physics. . . . Our experiences in science have taught us that nothing is more unfruitful than the maxim that at all costs one must produce something new. . . . The most important changes in the pattern of physical thinking can be seen most clearly in the *practical resistance* put up *against* these theories . . . it would be still more unreasonable to suppose that we ought to destroy all the old forms, and that the new will then already emerge of its own accord. . . . For only where the novel is forced upon us by the problem itself, where it comes in sense from outside ourselves, does it later have the power to transform. . . . *[Across the Frontiers]*

The idea of revolution in art still retains power as the legacy of Romanticism is incorporated into Modernism. But it loses its generativity as Modernism comes to serve the productive logic of the industrial system it initially repudiated, attempting to establish itself as a permanent tradition with its secret weapon, change for change's sake. When this dynamic is incorporated into creative capitalism it becomes further suspect, and when integrated into the context of climax inflation, it is positively fatal.

This ambivalence of revolutionism puts the inner contradictions of Post-Modernism into an intriguing perspective. For to the extent that the artist is to remain faithful to the revolution he meets no resistance, no authentic conservative or even official tradition which would define his challenge. Hence he ends up neither praised nor punished, neither *engagé* nor *degagé*. After all, how does one *change* something which is always in flux? Insofar as the artist subverts reality, it is only that of commercial reality screened by historicist facades, which in its contemporary multiplicity and transformational energy suggests a consciousness far more dominant than those textbook unities which Modernism presumably dispelled. The object of revolt is not some false unity or palpable reality, but the hypocritical screening process itself, a highbrow aesthetic dismemberment of lowbrow corporate convention. The anachronism and redundancy inherent in this revolutionism tend to throw the entire central nervous system of Post-Modernism out of whack.

In this context, it would seem obvious that a more conservative, historically oriented approach might modify a mindlessly protean Modernism. Modernism's distinction was, after all, to unsettle a historicist culture and clear away the remaining remnants of ecclesiastical and aristocratic establishments. It goes without saying that the Post-Modern must transcend an ahistorical culture and an audience whose presentness is given such a limited identity by mass communications and the Academy. This is already evident in the tendency of all Post-Modern arts to become historical commentaries on whatever genre they adopt. But this antidote has not achieved its predicted effect. What the textualists do to texts, rendering them "equal" in a historical vacuum of internalistic analysis, the conservative post-modernist tends to do to historical periods and styles. What we invariably end up with is a gesture of historical pathos without content, the restoration of historical images with no coordinates — a romanesque arch which holds up nothing, a Greek pilaster in mid air, a trapezoidal window in a neo-classical facade — the structural principle of which is a superimposition of images which refuse to dissolve with time, testimony not to a new eclecticism but merely the artist's erudition. What we have recently — in painting, music and architecture, no less than in literature, in opposition to an uncritical rejection of the past [can't go backness] — is an uncritical reception, an all-embracing nostalgia, in which *all* historical styles are dredged up simultaneously, history as gesture to a "pastness" which disguises the real pain of history and struggle for knowledge. The ideology of making it new becomes the ideology of making it (sort of) old. As Modernism has become the respectable culture, "tradition" becomes the Avant-Garde.

This is the real crux of the matter, and it is not to be avoided by demeaning this reconsideration as yet another "transitional" step. It would be a simple matter to drive the last nail in the coffin of Post-Modernism by merely pointing out the inadequacy of collage as overmediated technique, calculated contradiction as cuteness, ambiguity as refuge. In any event, literature has only begun to explore the wonderful possibilities of this ultra-eclecticism on a monumental scale, a pure ventriloquism without an individualized signature. The problem here is in the tendency of these violent adjacencies to a clownish jocularity; for to lay claim to and juxtapose all historical styles simultaneously is to rely, intentionally or not, on parody — a jest which conceals the problem. It is almost impossible to avoid such humor if the Post-Modern is in fact an uneasy amalgam of high modernism and popular culture, but what is required is not the easy playing off of a puritanical formalism against the comic strip images of Commercial Realism, but a continuity based on something more than intellectual revenge.

It is very 20th century to see the world in terms of systems. It is quite Modern to see all systems as prone to breakdown. It is the essence of Post-Modernism to define the system by its breaking point, to see the world as a humanly imposed system of distortion. This view confirms an art which increasingly denies any context of the actual, and a criticism whose jargon masks concrete conditions — both avoiding situations which normally elicit human response.

If we have failed to restore any tradition of objective reality, we can nevertheless question the enthronement of the dominant perceiver, to insist that if in fact he is in charge, he ought to make evident what the facts compel. If novelty is what we are after, then a change in thought patterns must be enforced, not only by the observer, but by the phenomena in question, a genuine excitement which is not generated by the easy reductions of a banal indeterminacy, but by the discovery of facts which no longer fit our theory. If we are still interested in "progress," this small modification of perspective, "the novel forced upon us by the problem itself," is absolutely crucial.

For all our anticipatory theories of change and mindless openendedness, there in fact remains a deadening slowness in the movement of ideas. Inflationary Post-Modernism chooses to be ignorant of a palpable extra-literary inertia. For what we have achieved is a culture bustling with activity and restlessness, and yet bewilderingly static. In one sense, this is nothing new. De Tocqueville noted that American society "appears animated because men and things are constantly changing; it is monotonous because all these changes are alike." But a new level of inconsequentiality is reached when all the arts are brought so willfully to the point of crisis by a subtle rhetoric of emptiness which suggests nothing so much as a furious stupor. The sense of the Post-Modern is quintessentially one of instability within immobility. In cultural matters, inflation abstracts anxiety, suspends judgment, multiplies interpretation, diffuses rebellion, debases standards, dissipates energy, mutes confrontation, undermines institutions, subordinates techniques, polarizes theory, dilates style, dilutes content, hyperpluralizes the political and social order while homogenizing culture. Above all, inflation masks stasis.

If we so heartily dismiss Realism because it trades upon a Positivistic world view, why do we then applaud contemporary work which also incorporates the pretensions of dated science — such as the entropy associated with closed heat machinery, or the systems theory already made obsolete by biochemistry and microprocessing? For every traditional enemy of plot, theme, character and story, we have a hackneyed anti-version of destabilization, indeterminism, defamiliarity and the artifice of knowledge. In one sense we are experiencing a new Primitivism; just as the caveman naively believed he was drawing something as it is, we accept and codify the distortions presumably determined by the structures of the mind.

The appeal of this autonomy appears incommensurable. Just as art as sanctuary was the final illusion of the Modernists, art as autonomy is the last gasp of Bourgeois individualism for the Post-Modernists. It vaguely ennobles; it assuages failure; it absolves everyone of accountability. In the guise of pure style, it masks an enormous deflation of aesthetic ego. It is an oddment of 20th century rhetoric that literary art should insist upon the absolution of autonomy at the very moment that its existence is most problematic. The vaunted fragmentation of art is no longer an aesthetic choice; it is simply a cultural aspect of the economic and social fabric. The artist who desires exemption from history finds himself merely crowded out. And in the Post-Modern world, it is not the artist but the audience which is fugitive.

Henri Matisse insisted that our senses have a "developmental age . . . not that of the immediate environment, but that of the period into which we were born . . . and it counts for more than anything that learning can give us." That sense of the senses is not congenial to our age; indeed the lack of it is what characterizes both our originality and fearfulness. We are convinced that our psychic mechanism is structured differently from that even of the most recent past; yet we can only define that difference in the most negative and categorical terms, with the notion that our *period* has done us in.

If we are to have a new literary history, it will have to deal with the new agencies of production, transmission, and administration of knowledge as dominant cultural institutions. It will have to be skeptical of all claims to autonomy, as well as the use of literature alone as a means of cultural, much less literary diagnosis. Quite as much as the natural sciences, such a history will have to modify its Modern evolutionary synthesis, and account for an art which is evolving in punctuational episodic fits and starts, a series of rapid and quirky mutations which do not move in the same direction at the same time. And above all in the case of the novel, it will have to confront the possibility that it has ceased "progressing"; that we are dealing in Post-Modern literature with something on the order of a large tree which has been radically pruned back to a shrub form, resulting in a profusion of lateral hybrid branchings from the parent stock, the most interesting of which seem, in the present lack of context, to lack any adaptive function. Long before science, literature discovered the fact that genetic structures are subject to leakage, that perpetuating material often undergoes spontaneous relocation. Temporal succession no longer implies static cluster, but only diversity without design.

What is most singular about Post-Modernism's ostensive enemies is not their profusion, but their abstraction. Consider Bloom's precursors, Gass's pseudo-artists, Bellow's professors, Trilling's students, Gardner's *immoralistes*; or consider the intractability which Barth ascribes to History and the Textualist imputes to language; the Left which predicates a conservative establishment based upon conspiracy, the Conservative who sees a Liberal establishment based upon betrayal: all testify to the dealignment of institutions, and the deterioration of an "official" culture, in which the increasing insignificance of literary or verbal suasion is only one aspect. The fact is that these adversaries are real punks. Our real enemies remain the old-fashioned, intractable ones: concentrations of economic and political power which have become inflexible; careerism and boredom; the cynicism of the producer of cultural goods, and the genuine bewilderment of the consumer. The Post-Modern cannot blame its lack of momentum on any particularized resistance, but rather upon an incomplete mobilization of its own scattered resources. This constitutes the potential for a mentality which truly deserves a new name — an art without scapegoats.

We are dealing here with some genuine historical mysteries. What happened to that newly sophisticated and enthusiastic literate public created within distinct memory by the explosion of higher education, the new pedagogy, and the enthusiastic assimilation of foreign cultures? The one characteristic of *all* national inflations in the 20th century is the relative pauperization of the intellectual middle class. (It is to miss the point to say they probably deserve it.)

Further, no one has adequately explained the enormous range of voice, the multiplicity of mode available to the writer in the last thirty years. It cannot be accounted for by "the breakdown" of traditional values, any more than by "the rise" of some mutagenous intelligence. Explanations which are not pleasant to face are (1) that epistemological nihilism begets an unrestricted licentiousness of expression; (2) that unprecedented proliferation in art is energized not by demand but by total indifference; and (3), most unsettling of all, that freedom of expression seems to lack power without resistance, principled or otherwise.

In short, there seems to be a relationship between the inflation and proliferation of artistic modes, a culture which places so many modalities at the consumer's disposal that none of them have more importance than another, and agencies of transmission of knowledge which emphasize intellectual activity so conventional that it can have no decisive value. Whoever comes to grips with this will be a great fiction writer, and tangentially testify to the fact that the traditions of Formalism and Realism do not make much sense when invoked as mere "first principles."

To comprehend the Post-Modern is to sense a striking reversal of energy. The velocities of change inherent in institutional agencies of transmission, whether critical or commercial, have become culturally dominant. In short, *attitudes toward art change more dynamically than art itself*: we move from History of Ideas to Hermeneutics in little more than a generation. Post-Modern means the first culture in history totally under the control of 20th century technology, and the first in five hundred years in which information is codified in ways which do not depend on literacy. All we have discovered, thanks largely to mass communications, is that "reality" is often more hollow than its verbal configuration, and that meaning *dates* even faster than style.

There seems to be no question that the central dynamics of Modernism provide a diminishing return. The Avant-Garde has lost any sense of historical relation, the solipsistic impulse has frittered away its detachment and pathos, eclecticism has become timid and defensive, and the cutting edge of Nihilistic perplexity is increasingly translated as mere articles of bad faith, spawning only yet another of America's mindless religious revivals. The prevailing mood is a *nice* negativism, a sweet nihilism which not only forbids itself any faith in progress, but in negation itself, since that would require a firmly held position. In its nostalgia for the rock-solid alienation of Modernism, it views the universe as a relative pudding.

This often reflects the belief that we are becoming more conservative. Not exactly. We are simply losing our faith in irony as the primary convention of aesthetic behavior. We are, in other words, just beginning to develop an emotional revision of Modernism's faith in the technocracy of art, a uniquely difficult task, since Modernism's seignory resembles nothing so much as that of the American Empire — extending its hegemony in the apparently sincere belief that it does not constitute one, because it is open-ended.

* * *

With the insouciance of a Virginia Woolf, let us periodize Post-Modernism within the velocity of the money supply, which began rising in the spring of 1946, accelerated in the late fifties, peaked in 1969 as the Great Society demanded both a foreign war and a domestic slumber party, continued out of control throughout the seventies, and began to subside only in the summer of 1981, as, one by one, the myths of inflation began to be brutally dismantled. It is no accident that the outcry of intellectuals traces this trajectory perfectly — from whine to scream to wheeze. What "ripples," what "trickles down" in this process is not patrimony but futility. And despite the eccentricity of the metaphor, I expect the dates will hold well enough in retrospect.

Consider: the false productivity of inflation coextensive with the exaggerated dynamism of art, the notion of every *accelerating value* as the dominant cultural illusion, masking the progressive devaluation of successive intellectual tenders; art and its explication as a growth industry dependent upon constant innovation, but finally unable to bear the weight of its capriciously accumulated technical apparatus, so that it ends up expressing only the loss of both personal and social mastery. Is there not something in the cavalier profligacy as well as the undeniable and anxious ambition of Post-Modern writing which is highly suggestive of printing currency you don't have? Add to this the relentless flight from all values, whatever their category, which makes Dada look like child's play; and the transfer of wealth to the most centralized agencies, reflecting what Keynes quaintly called the "superior political influence of the debtor class."

Modernism begins in opposition to this class, but reaches its apotheosis in the context of European Totalitarianism, where the fragmentation of the "official" narrative becomes obligatory as the primary act of human resistance. But the Modernism which began as the destruction of the Bourgeois worldview becomes the Bourgeois idiom *par excellence*, a kind of mass produced and ready made surrealism — familiar images in unfamiliar contexts — images which are not juxtaposed as much as they are simply disconnected from their source: the Avant-Garde as spectator sport, the Picasso in the corporate courtyard, Modernism as the new Bourgeois Realism.

This most recent false consciousness is given its tone not by the arrogance of blind progress, but by the arrogance of a demystification which is Everyman's prerogative — casual subversion as false sophistication and short term legitimation. Both social and literary revolt are dissipated as they find association in movements and fashions which are integrated as techniques into the social order — a trade unionization of intellect no less self-deluding because it calls itself an *epistéme*. And as the anarchic impulse is diffused through technique, all revolutionary gestures take on the element of burlesque — which accounts for the peculiar humor of contemporary literature. We seem incapable of making the simple distinction between Modernism as one of the many available traditions, and pure ecstatic response. Through its obsession with counter-genre, preferring parody to confrontation, Post-Modernism tends to change all *politics* into *mystiques*, and increasingly substitutes the idea of posterity for that of engagement. It purifies the future as Modernism tried to decontaminate the past.

From the man so rooted in the actual as to be "provincial," the

Bourgeois by ingesting Modernism is able to turn all experience, no matter how unsettling, into a form of consumption, so that the aesthetic experiment *is* the social experiment. Art can neither consecrate nor oppose because it is the norm. Every contemporary artist becomes *sui generis* by default. The first task of the Post-Modern writer becomes the necessity of somehow fighting his way through the Autonomy of Technique.

Ours is a melancholy history of fiat money, of a culture which did not squander its patrimony as much as it believed it could profit from constant devaluation. Indeed the only thing which prevented us from veering into hyperinflation was a large and strong middle class which finally acted to prevent further confiscation of its savings. To call this a "conservative" act is as crude as identifying overexpansion of credit with liberalism. It was simply an act of reflexive self-preservation upon which conservatives capitalized politically. It is silly to be even remotely partisan in this case, as both the right and the left have followed the same policy in our lifetime — go for growth, and when you can't grow, fake it through inflation, buy gains through deficits, and ignore, even to this day, the massive loss of real wealth the nation has suffered in the last twenty years.

Art, like all non-market activity, suffers when the spread between the cost of money and the real rate of return is excessive. It suffers further of course from the conservative "pay as you go" syndrome, as well as the liberal's penchant to defensively link aesthetic progress with some kind of safety net for the economically disadvantaged. Contemporary American literature in this sense is given much of its tone, like classical studies before it, as the province of an economically superfluous and politically dysfunctional academic proletariat.

In short, the function of art is radically diffused when the culture refuses, as an operative principle, any longer term horizon for itself. The most perfidious legacy of inflation was to volatilize and compress investment and credit cycles as well as the movement of all received ideas, a malarial asymmetry in which the larger players who once provided long term stability also became short term traders, relying on short term hot money for their capital base and squaring the ledger by frantic overnight borrowing — as true for the Academy as for Citicorp.

The stock market in less than a generation becomes dominated by the largest institutions (75% of all trades) who turn over their portfolios at an unprecedented rate (based on a quarterly return), even though this increased velocity results in performance no better than the historical averages. This only accentuates non-productive exchanges within the economic order, a market which has become interiorized, "self-conscious," if you will.

Moreover, the recent move from a relatively regulated and redistributive economy to one more aggressively market-driven does not result in a longer term investment horizon, but in fact only formalizes the obsession with maximizing short term return. The consequence is institutional competition for both credit and liquidity which further excludes the smaller player and heralds the appearance of an increasingly two-class society — one in which only the affluent can achieve significant gains.

One effect of volatility and the compression of cycles, of an entire culture of short-term traders, is to make any extrapolative thinking look foolish, whether it takes place in social relations, economic planning, or even novels. This effect is further exacerbated by unprecedented indebtedness.* Indebtedness creates excessive caution, not principled conservatism. It manifests itself in social indifference, cultural shoddiness, petty chauvinism, and above all, political timidity — primary characteristics of the Eighties. Insofar as there are any overviews, they tend to take on the polarization and wild oscillations of the Realist/Formalist debate — intellectual doom and gloomers vs. the self-serving optimists of the "opportunity society."

It is a commonplace that no politician has the courage to recommend a program of retrenchment and shared sacrifice. Where would he look for a model of self-discipline? The corporate boardroom? The bureaucracy? Our labor unions or religious leaders? The Academy, God help us? The basic assumption which still permeates the culture is that we must inflate or die. And, in fact, the only interest in stabilization seems to be to restrict borrowing now, so that we will be able to reflate later when the recovery aborts.

But while the effects of climax inflation will define the culture far into the future, inflation as a working hypothesis, as a governing metaphor, has probably run its course. If art is in any sense "ahead" of its culture, then certainly recent literature anticipates considerably

---

*As of this writing, public and private interest payments are equivalent to 25% of the national income, and individual private debt is five times as large as that of the Treasury — which itself is a net debtor in the world economy, financed in effect by poorer foreign countries.

lessened expectations as well as a legitimate longing for the modestly concrete.

The only thing we know for sure about long term economic cycles is that they endure long enough to erase the memories of those in power. No one alive is experienced in the politics of deflation. Nor is there much cognizance of the fact that the changes we are undergoing are structural and not cyclical, to the extent that all conventional techniques, *both* stimulation and restraint, may be inadequate to sustained recovery. This fact is underscored by the Orwellian euphemisms we have recently developed. Calling relentlessly falling prices "disinflation" is like referring to bank failures as "financial accidents" or loans which will never be paid off as "non-performing." What we are presently experiencing *is* historically unique — a simultaneous deflation in commodities, inflation hedges, and a moribund manufacturing base — together with continued high inflation in the increasingly dominant service sector of the economy. This is a situation, needless to say, to which all our conventional statistical indices and measuring techniques, much less our ideologies, are irrelevant.

Deflation is after all simply a matter of credit liquidation, the recognition that you can no longer pay off your debt with cheaper dollars. The value of cash rises relative to all real goods. What happens is simply that one's collateral is no longer sufficient to cover one's debt service — there could be no more poignant description of much Post-Modern art — a phenomenon typical of a culture which lacks not diversity or ambition but liquidity throughout the system. By contrast with the euphoria which preceded the Depression, the peculiar fate of the Post-Modern is that we cannot say that we lack sufficient information, that we have not received the necessary signals: rather, we are paralyzed by the obvious.

We must bear in mind that it may well be more difficult to restore confidence after inflation than after a crash. Conventional capitalist wisdom has always dictated that survival is based upon identifying the primary trend and not fighting it. But in an age when an entire culture behaves as short term speculators, then it is the velocity rather than the direction of the trend which is most significant. When one has been accustomed to accommodating unprecedented velocities of change, when one has profited by discounting all values in advance, the final result is a terminal loss of direction. In other words, in art as the marketplace, when all bets are hedged and everyone is overextended, paying a premium for the inflation which *must* continue if indebtedness is to be paid off with debased currency, the consequence is a *fear of stability* — as assets have been fully pledged to declining value. It is this progressive erosion of borrower's collateral, the hype finally come home to roost, which has become a likely scenario, a peculiarly American squeeze in which any return to sanity induces panic.

The Post-Modern survived for a while on lost positions, thrived initially on the wonderful sloppiness of a culture ready for anything, celebrating discontinuities until the excitement of dislocation and the explosions of scale began to wane, and hopelessly inflated expectations gave way to a culture clearly out of control. Within the Hell's gate of the 20th century, it thrived upon a period of capitalism which had no memory of instability or stagnation, and was able to play at the dangerous life. It struck not against the rigidities of culture, but made fun of the culture's ability to digest and regurgitate anything. It did not see that this resiliency was finally based upon the most profound indifference and poignant confusion; its signature was in signifying well in advance that it was going to break all the rules. The Post-Modern has no experience with truly repressive cultural institutions. Hence, it fostered a revolution without an enemy. News known is news discounted.

In short, what began as a discontinuous aggregate of forms and processes which appeared to be independent, ended up as a blinding succession of temporary cultures, disseminated by increasingly centralized agencies, in which the economic calculus of profitability was the only criterion. The culture which developed was defined solely by its markets — the intellectual corollary of which is *category* — and markets, as some unliterary sage observed, are there to fool you, not to lead you.

The primary characteristic of this centralized power was no longer blind accumulation but calculated evanescence. An overmediated Modernism became less an antidote than a stimulus to an overprocessed culture. Literature refused to see that in such a situation, it remained, in spite of itself, a conservatory force. It could not step back from the experiment for fear of being branded reactionary. And so we ended up with a most simple-minded Conservatism, justifiable only as a Draconian reaction to inflation; a tacit acceptance of all the Modernist clichés together with a literal revivalism in which equilibrium could be envisioned only as a return to "basic values," every one of which Modernism puts into question.

Neo-Conservatism has failed to offer a rigorous rationalism or even an avuncular Neo-Classicism to counter Modernism's Formalist aestheticism. To counter the Formalist bias through Literal Revivalism is exactly like trying to control inflation through rigid monetarism — to restrict supply through the imposition of standards which no one can agree how to locate, much less enforce. While skeptical of unbridled self-realization in art, the Neo-Conservative accepts it unequivocally in economic activity, and as a consequence fosters a politics free of moral and practical justification. He promulgates Modernist attitudes insofar as they accelerate technological progress, capitalistic creativity and hierarchical administration, and in this sense definitively defuses the explosive content of the Modernist revolution.

To all the uncertainties of the century, inflation adds the question of what the future will buy. Even the most privileged and/or astute cannot locate a store of value which is not anxiety producing, and dispossession is so generalized that it cannot be blamed upon any *class*, because self-interest can no longer be rationally determined. To argue for a centrality of values in a culture in which all forces are exponentially centrifugal has its charm, but to bewail the lack of standards in a society in which institutions fail to preserve their integrity is simply to refuse reality. The history of Modernism is the history of the failure to recreate a moral dimension in the culture by aesthetic means alone. A return to a new aesthetic probity is not likely to affect the puerility of our politics. Certainly, the situation will not be ameliorated by a return to an intellectual gold standard of Modernism.

The classic conservative defense of the "free market" is that its failures are the consequence of an incomplete application of its principles, complicated by a cabal of collectivist elitists. Yet the entire period of Modernism was paralleled, in all the varied cultures it affected, by a variety of broadly based spontaneous and pragmatic countermeasures, by those who felt the elementary requirements of social and artistic life were threatened by the ever expanding market mechanism. To ignore the scope of this intervention is to be saddled with the supreme 19th century fiction that markets arise spontaneously to satisfy human needs, as well as to ignore the cell by cell dissolution caused by inflation, the ebbing faith in *all* institutions, non-profit and commercial alike.

The Modernist revolt was in large measure directed against markets dominated by petit Bourgeois national chauvinism, and was made possible by the remnants of aristocratic salon capitalism. It should not be surprising that Post-Modernism, faced with markets dominated by the multinational corporation, should have capitalized upon the patronage of universities and museums, or that we should be nostalgic for the remarkable interventionist spirit of Modernism — an art which, in retrospect at least, eventually made its own market.

A chief irony of the inflationary Post-Modern era is that it provides historically unprecedented employment for intellectuals within a broader market offering a decreasing demand for their services. As a consequence, intellectuals have learned how to create jobs for themselves but not how to *intervene* effectively in the market. This is the most banal but basic contradiction in the mythology of autonomy. But while the self-protectionism of the contemporary American artist is indisputable, his shortcomings are not likely to be ameliorated by the "magic" of the marketplace, any more than a sterile Formalism is to be amplified by some "magic" realism.

It is fascinating to ponder how the Realist/Formalist debate echoes the holistic antinomies of the Free Market vs. Interventionist worldviews. The Interventionist maintains, as the Avant-Garde does, that the market represents a status quo which must be leveraged or subverted, depending on your politics, so that in the Formalist sense, values must be incorporated into a system devoid of values, and that in the end such values will *somehow* come to constitute an inwardly coherent and self-correcting mechanism.

The Freemarketeer, on the other hand, justifies the status quo precisely because it is devoid of extra-market values, emphasizing with the Realist that objective truth can only be achieved through reciprocity, the interaction of autonomous, self-interested activities which also *somehow* come to constitute an equilibrium. The Neo-Conservative wants his art simple, with its values up front, a governance which it descries in the social sphere. The Interventionist wants to project values into the social mechanism, but rebels when they are imposed upon art.

On the face of it, these are two of the more balefully speculative and basically crazy notions in the history of ideas. The hypothetical resolution in both cases cannot be understood apart from the adjustment process which leads to it, yet in both cases this process is celebrated as not only "invisible," but somehow altogether fitting. It is very contemporary to want values, as long as they are in the other guy's bailiwick.

Anyone with a residue of common sense knows that the economy or its productive relations cannot be understood except through some subjective amalgam of both Free Market and Interventionist praxis, that neither model alone can take into account normative human behavior, much less explain the mystery of the dynamic process it postulates. Likewise, no work of fiction, or the apparatus which heaves it into the world, can be understood, much less produced, in terms of Formalist or Realist exclusivity.

The neo-conservative critique is valuable in that it grants perspective to the looseness of the Adversary style, and obviates the great blindspot of the liberal left — that economic and aesthetic freedom are conspicuously related. In an inflationary era, it is necessary to emphasize that benefits are in fact based to some extent on value produced, and that real productivity must somehow be determined and rewarded. Yet this is not likely to be accomplished by a perverse combination of Manchester Liberalism, Social Darwinism and Kantian epistemology, the removal of the weak sisters by the big brothers from the free market, or the notion that the rich will save us if we only let them. The final irony of the neo-conservative is that he reasserts the predominance of the free market at the exact historical point in which the ability of free markets to control inflation collapsed.

This represents no conspiracy, but only another missed opportunity. Neo-conservatism has refused to insist on the accountability either of producer or consumer; nor has it recognized the extent to which third party agencies of transmission have annulled the traditional transactional relationship of buyer and seller, reader and writer, perceiver and perceived. It represents a vision of both social and aesthetic experience which conveniently leaves the corporation, the market maker, out of the equation. It has refused to mount an attack upon the aesthetic utopianism of modern art and its scruffy live-in lover, that dominant perceiver who has come to exist solely on the junk food of ecumenicism. Its defense of realism has not reasserted the tradition of reciprocal or objective truth, but only bought into the literal as an aspect of consumer culture. Hence, we have a commercialism screened by historicist facades, a rationalism which is defined ultimately only by the profit motive.

Just as the conservative blindly equates Modernism with progress, the Formalist all too often equates anti-modernism with the reactionary — so that he revolts not against a narrow vision of experience, but against the hypocritical screening process of literal revivalism through the formulaic counter-genre. In neither case is a palpable reality either engaged or refuted. A fiction which challenges only its own aesthetic conventions becomes as suspect as one which pretends to be a direct reflection of reality, just as an x-ray can be quite as boring as a mirror.

Formalism and Realism have lost both their finiteness *and* their history. They are no longer conflicting theories, competing modes of inquiry, historical traditions, opposed realities, or even definitive styles — only programs to be punched into.

What we have undergone is a kind of "digitalization" of American literature, which is not so much the binary reduction of complex experience into computer sets of ones and zeros, but what Kierkegaard meant when he said "our age has attained an unparalleled interest in forgery — in doing the highest things by leaping over the immediate steps." This is expressed in Formalist/Realist debate as a self-perpetuating oscillating series of cherished and hated selves; a classic illustration of schizophrenic activity.

In any event, the Post-Modern ended, as all aesthetic movements must, when it could provide no values as an alternative to the market-place — for the mysterious force of all serious art is the extent to which it always exceeds the requirements of the market.

There will be two obvious and legitimate objections to this line of argument. The first is that while it's all well and good to point out cultural determinism in the abstract, no practitioner really takes such ideas seriously when struggling with an expedient like, say, a novel — even given the seemingly unquenchable appetite of Post-Modernism for the problem which *looks* philosophical. But it is wrong to think that because there is no cultural centrality, there are no strong cultural predispositions. I have tried to suggest that the contemporary writer's options of subject matter and technique are largely objectified by confused attitudes towards History, Adversary, Audience and Genre — the weight and absence of each — and more, that these notions are independent of his perceptions of the "market," much less his "creative soul."

Second, there will be the caveat that economics is too blunt an instrument for cultural, much less literary, analysis. I will go further and suggest that the basic sense of Post-Modern culture is *essentially economic*; that in fact, the *only* governing coherence of the period derives from the fact that it provided the western industrialized democracies with a unique ahistorical interlude of peace and prosperity, as well as the illusion of an infinitely sustainable growth and accelerating value — and more, that when such economic progressiveness is gradually eroded, the entire culture disintegrates. Inflation is reflected in late capitalism not as political havoc but as cultural anomie. Unlike Modernism, which thrived in a period of economic and political upheaval, Post-Modernist art takes its dynamism from a relatively classless society which asks "why shouldn't I get mine?" — the aesthetic and intellectual corollary of which is an art based upon "hey, why not?" — a program which is virtually guaranteed self-destruction, insofar as it refuses to acknowledge the increasing disparity between resources and expectations in both artist and audience.

In this context we can see that several of Modernism's time-honored legacies have been brought to an abrupt and deservedly wretched conclusion.

The single legacy of Modernism which remains discernably Humanist was the idea of art as permanent — perhaps the only permanence. We are well aware by now that art does not endure — what survives is largely a matter of luck and extra-artistic activity. This in itself accounts for the self-deprecation and defensive arrogance inextricably entwined in most contemporary aesthetic gestures.

Second, Modernism's emphasis on the exposure of artifice, its assumption that art ought to be reduced to its constituent elements, that the functionalist mode which dissects all things into its parts somehow clears the air, has been perversely long-lived. A great deal has been bared, but nothing has been cleared up.

Third, Post-Modernism rehearses the cycle of European Modernism in an Americanized version. For Modernism begins with the cauterization of a facile 19th-century liberalism, and ends with the despair of failed revolution. It is Post-Modernism's peculiar ambiance that it registers a progressive disillusionment with successive aesthetic liberations as it pursues them; its dirty little secret is that Demystification does not finally alleviate either human or aesthetic problems, but seems only to deepen and further conceal them.

Fourth, the Post-Modernist generation is the first in America to experience both institutional support and control of the arts, the first to experience an "official" mass culture, and the corporate bureaucratic mind-set which accompanies it. It's no accident that this experience parallels the ascendancy of the American Empire and our quite brief, as it turns out, Age of Perfectability. Ours is the first American generation without predictable social prejudices about art, a benign tolerance which eventually tends to empty art of any social value. The defensiveness inherent in the autonomous stance only reminds us finally of the lack of societal support. Art has lost its entitlements. It is the utter fragility, not the autarky of cultural institutions which is the Post-Modern subject.

Finally, let us bid farewell to those two most elusive historical personages, the Vanguardiste and the Bourgeois, who have washed each other's hands for more than a century, a stormy but enduring mutual accommodation which thrived on all the strengths and disabilities of Modernism. Heroic Modernism's certitudes were the expression not of a doctrine but of a faith in the dialectics of oppositionism. Far from synthesizing these antinomies — serious and popular, genre and counter-genre, style and content, etc. — Post-Modernism only further ironizes, and finally parodies them.

In this sense, such antinomies continue to represent the intellectual's preferred escapism, insofar as they permit the illusion that a *series* of rotating autonomous states offer real alternatives, yet another confusion of cyclical with structural change. Fiction cannot afford to play this game. Literature can again resonate with experience, not by adopting some new external imperative, which in any event the consciousness industry will invent for it anew each morning, but by a faithful rededication to its own peculiar generic constitution, its lack of an ontology, and the consequent cross-processing which defies autonomy — a practical energy which can never be systematic, but cannot fail to be inclusive. For if fiction does not aim for the inclusive, it degenerates with astonishing rapidity into that most febrile of literary forms — prose poetry.

Fiction, in short, is Modern man's method by which antinomies can be *unlearned*; a process in which oppositions are neither resolved nor transcended but made reciprocally evocative. Pluralism is not relativism. The many languages of Babel are not nonsense; only different languages awaiting conflation. And the truth of fiction is not indeterminate — only a set of facts which cannot be presumptively inferred from other facts, which is thus unlikely to find expression as a coherent theory.

The final contradiction which lies at the heart of Post-Modern literature remains our fundamental inability to acquire a non-relative vantage point for observing the world. Yet the fiction writer perforce assumes an epistemologically privileged position, even as he may assert that it is impossible. The fact that our knowledge is based on a contingent and finite position in the world, that the aesthetic act is not empirically invincible, is not by this time exactly a world-shaking discovery.

Certainly, there seem no two centuries as discontiguous as the 19th and the 20th. If Modernist innovation seems perverse in its tyranny of originality, was not its predecessor also something of an extreme anomaly? In Ortega's words, "the exclusive realism of the 19th century is an unparalleled monstrosity . . . situating the center of gravity of the work in the Human. That is why the New Art, so extravagant in appearance, rejoins, in at least one sense, the Royal road of Art. This road is called the 'Will to Style.' " That road we are still on, always palliated by both commercial and critical fashion, which share and more often than not dominate the same thoroughfare. It is an uncomfortably short step from *Style Moderne* to "life-style," that consumer view that life offers the freedom once reserved for art — without art's arbitrary exactitudes.

Modernism did not cause our famous "liquidation of literary values." It simply presided over the end of describing all arts and intellectual disciplines in literary terms. Language, as Foucault reminds us, did not "return to the field of thought until the late 19th century," when literary grammars of discourse began to be replaced by technical languages in all intellectual disciplines. The 20th century is an irruptive open site characterized by a radical reflection upon language, and the tendency of all disciplines to assert their autonomy and supremacy by an increasingly technical commentary upon their own procedures. But this once exciting pluralist disputation has by this time degenerated into a monolithic linguistic determinism as our central revisionist commonplace, displacing any sense of literariness as a *natural* aspect of human cognition, and banishing the novelistic from human experience.

Fiction may be linguistic, but as language works it tends to disappear, to escape its linguistic constitution. There is always a moment when language wins itself away from its entanglements and drives on to its proper due. The "problem" of fiction does not grow out of a defect in language, but in false dogmatizing models which assume language to be autonomous or frozen, rather than a disclosing agent, a problem which always arises when a static model is applied to a dynamic process. An inflationary culture only further distorts the potential for any partial equilibrium.

If we have learned anything it is that art can proceed with considerable enthusiasm in the knowledge that if truth does not exist in nature, it can exist as a provisional insight, internally consistent and pragmatically verifiable. In Jacques Rivière's words: "For the writer, will not true precision consist in gathering up the word, inscribing it where it appears, accepting its fortuitous value; seizing its testimony without worrying about its aberration . . .?" Fiction can take its stand, as Science itself does, in celebrating the particularity of partial knowledge.

By playing off the amplitude of technique against the paucity of spirit, by capitalizing upon the lack of relations between intellectual production and the economy of life, Post-Modernism brings the cultural inflation of Modernism to an attenuated conclusion, neither bang nor whimper. It is a postlude which cannot be completed — but only peters out arbitrarily and inconclusively, suffering no resistance save that of its own lack of momentum. For all its frivolity it suggests nothing so much as the tear which will not flow — a *horror vaccui*.

Post-Modernism constitutes its own aura — which we might call the Hypothetical Apocalyptic — based on the apprehension that we have bought too much time, on time; that only a climactic washout can correct the distortions of the last twenty years, as well as allay the increasingly legitimate fear that the ongoing turmoil may provoke an authoritarian reaction. There is the overwhelming sense that the culture is at a breaking point, that we will not be permitted the graduated painless decay so admirable in the *fin de sieclè*. This is the inevitable consequence of cultural inflation, the self-feeding expectation of a society which must ever increase consumption in order to absorb continual devaluation, a psychology which has been analyzed only in terms of the consumer but never in terms of the anxiety of the producer of cultural goods. This anxiety has a distinctly unliterary ambiance, but it is underscored in literature by the fact that the rhetoric of crisis has played itself out, that we have been denied the conventional climacterics of history, that we have run out of deaths, that we are undergoing real debacles and not projecting them in advance.

Permanent crisis is a Modernist mood; it gains both power and perspective from the sense of a culture coming to a close and another fast approaching, the clinching of the merger of Modernism and Americanism. The permanent crisis was gratifying not because it held out hope, but because, given its own internal dynamic of detente, it had nothing to lose. Thus, Post-Modernism reflects not a radical uncertainty so much as an unconsidered suspension of judgment. Insofar as there is a crisis, it is not one of style, nor intellectual feasibility, and it is certainly not *linguistic*. The crisis is largely institutional, and that would not be so significant were there nothing in our aestheticized history which prepared us to perceive a crisis in institutional terms. This perception will not affect the quality of a single sentence in American literature. But sometimes we must acknowledge a cultural actuality which has no short term aesthetic consequences, indeed no necessary consequences whatsoever.

Would it be presumptuous to suggest that there is already a writing in the making which chooses not to tussle with Modernist orthodoxy, which does not see the necessity of "putting distance" between itself and the canons of the recent past, which fears neither reciprocity nor continuity even if it cannot yet claim them — and which is not embarrassed by the likely suspicion that there are vast areas of experience untouched by Literary Modernism? No doubt such a relinquishment will be seen as a cowardly retreat. Because of our obsession with system and category, we believe that ideas can only be supplanted by others — "the consolation," says Nietzsche, "that the first nature was once a second, and that every conquering second nature becomes a first." But ideas can also simply subside, succumb to their own essential toxicity. We always underestimate the cleansing power of *inertia* — the despair of the Avant-Garde and Realist reformer alike.

Yet here the Post-Modern might offer some small perspective, if little consolation. For taken together in all their patent oppositionism, the 19th and 20th centuries represent not simply another unresolved split, but the potentiality of an extraordinarily rich, nurturing, complex tradition — suggesting that all our antecedents are finally ours; that the writer might have a number of entirely different perspectives within his lifetime; indeed, a number of careers within a single work, within the sentence itself. If the Post-Modern were capable of setting itself an obvious task, it would be the recombinancy of 19th century emotional generosity with the technical virtuosity of the 20th. The most astonishing writers of our time — Nabokov, Grass, many of the Latin Americans — are not so much defined by their "extra-territoriality," but by the fact that their Modernism came to them modified and clarified by other strong literary and cultural traditions.

It remains the wonder of literature that it can provide a rich patrimony without identifiable or even worthy parents. And it is the peculiar privilege of this generation not to salvage the best of the past, or to hedge the future, but to rethink what has been jettisoned in the name of a spurious purity — to question what is, in fact, *expendable*. Only then, by attention to those areas of experience *re*mystified by Modernism's incessantly circular destruction of aesthetic conventions, conventions which in our generation were rarely mastered, much less experienced, can the not yet dead be said to be living.

"I am finite once and for all," says William James, "and all the categories of my sympathy are knit up with the finite world, and with things which have a history . . . I have neither eyes nor ears nor heart nor mind for anything of an opposite description, and the stagnant felicity of the Absolute's own perfection moves me as little as I move it."

The Post-Modern era, which began so admirably as the refutation of a sterile continuity, is suffused with the discovery that far from having put Modernism in abeyance, it retains its most salient and questionable features. Insofar as society is unwilling to change art with any acountability, art remains self-validating by default. Insofar as art challenges the norms of the market, it is always justified by its "essence," rather than by any value it might impart to life. To forget such cultural idolatry is now the precondition for any creative thought.

It was Franz Kafka who anticipated, as with so much else, the figure of the Post-Modern artist. "You must push your head through the wall,'' he says. ''It is not difficult to penetrate, for it is made of the thinnest stuff. But *what is difficult* is not to let yourself be deceived by the fact that there is already an extremely deceptive painting on the wall showing you pushing yourself through it.''

This is the unflattering portrait of the portrait of the contemporary artist, his head stuffed through the cultural proscenium, only his ass on view for those who are obliged to stake out the real. We do not know whether this odd posture is due to his emulation or his avoidance of his official portrait, whether this is a willed breakthrough or simply the momentary inattention of a troubled man; a reflexive imitation, or a desperate escape from a ridiculously limited identity. We suspect that, in his ungainliness, questions about whether he is completing the revolution or laying the ground for a new sensibility are of some indifference to him, that he has limited energy to make further *claims* for art, particularly when the instructions for technical subversion are so precise, the barriers so porous, and equivocation so apparently profitable. We do not even know whether this is supposed to be funny, but we suspect that humor which must call attention to itself as humor is not exactly humor — it suggests more, a deep and uncomprehending fear.

What we do know is that the central question of this late hour of the century, a question in which the social, political and aesthetic at last lose their autonomy, can no longer be avoided. Once through the wall, what then? How is the banality of revolution to be itself subverted?

Beyond the sheetrock of Modernism lies fire; a fire built largely from books; a fire to which we must summon the nerve to consign our own.